HITLER

HITLER

Wyndham Lewis

Foreword by

John Chapman

ANTELOPE HILL PUBLISHING

Hitler
By Wyndham Lewis
Originally published 1931, University of California

Republished 2020 Antelope Hill Publishing
Second printing 2022

The content of this work is in the public domain.

Foreword Copyright © 2020 John Chapman

Cover art by sswifty
Edited by Tom Simpson
Formatted by Margaret Bauer

Antelope Hill Publishing
www.antelopehillpublishing.com

Hardcover ISBN-13: 978-1-953730-28-2
Paperback ISBN-13: 978-1-953730-20-6
EPUB ISBN-13: 978-1-953730-11-4

Es ist kein ausweg: wenn ihr versinkt, so versinkt die Menschheit mit, ohne Hoffnung einer einstigen Wiederherstellung.

There is no way out: if you sink, your humanity sinks with you, without any hope of restoration to your former glory.

(From Fichte's *Addresses to the German Nation*)

CONTENTS

Foreword by John Chapman   ix

PART I
BERLIN

1. The Weimar Republic and the *Dritte Reich*   3
2. Berlin *im Licht*   9
3. The Berlin "Eldorado"   15

PART II
ADOLF HITLER—THE MAN AND THE PARTY

1. The Oneness of "Hitlerism" and of Hitler   21
2. Hitlerism and the *Judenfrage*   24
3. Adolf Hitler a Man of Peace   30
4. Hitler an "Armed Prophet"   35

PART III
RACE AND CLASS

1. Many Class Wars   45
2. *The Art of Being Ruled*   51
3. One Advantage in Race-Notion   55

PART IV

YOUTH-MOVEMENT BECOMES "HITLER-MOVEMENT"   59

PART V
"ALL THAT IS NOT RACE IN THIS WORLD IS DROSS"

1. *Blutsgefühl* — 67
2. Analysis of the Exotic Sense — 74
3. The Fox and the Goose — 80
4. "Aryanism" in Politics and "Diffusionism" in Anthropology — 85
5. Aryan Hegemony and a Germanic *Volapuk?* — 90

PART VI
HITLERIST ECONOMICS

1. War-Debts—And the Great Creditor-Nation, America — 95
2. Choosing Your Change — 101
3. Are You a "Credit-Crank"? — 105
4. Credit-Crankery Rampant — 107
5. The Two Antagonistic Capitalisms — 113
6. Misery-Spot, or Golden Age? — 118

PART VII

CONCLUSION — 125

FOREWORD

Lewis and Hitler, Parallel Lives

By: John Chapman

Adolf Hitler, to quote Gustave Aimard, "is the idea whose time has come and hour struck." If one were to paraphrase a more famous Frenchman, that of Voltaire, one might say if Adolf Hitler did not exist, it would be necessary to invent him. So ubiquitous and fascinating Adolf Hitler has been that even when reduced to a one-dimensional caricature that makes the Devil look sheepish, science fiction writers of time travel stories find it necessary to spare him in their own works as Hitler is the Atlas carrying the postmodern world, its technological development, and its morality on his shoulders. Students within community college philosophy 101 classes might brag about having the bravery of killing baby Hitler, but there's no doubt they would blink at the prospect of losing the one man that defines their entire existence.

Time Magazine has earned eternal enmity for once naming Adolf Hitler their Man of the Year. Their only error was in not naming him the Man of the Century (the winner was Albert Einstein, with runners-up being Gandhi and Franklin Delano Roosevelt). Under their own rules for Man of the Year, it was meant to signify who was the most consequential person in that year, independent of morality. They rarely ever get it right, but they got it right there, even if they couched it in descriptions later discarded by the magazine's detractors that described Hitler as the "greatest threatening force that the democratic, freedom-loving world faces today." There is no argument to be had. Hitler was the most consequential person of the twentieth century and if the zeitgeist is anything to go by then he should already be on the twenty-first century's shortlist despite being dead seventy-five years.

Hitler is not a man who invites indifference. The only way to have no opinion is to have no opinions. For those who shape society and sentiment, however, moral disgust suffices in place of thought. What cannot be denied—not by traumatized Jews, not by agitated liberals, and not even by milquetoast critics of the right—is that the mystique of Hitler is something both ethereal and extraordinary. Savitri Devi, the forerunner of the spiritual view of Hitler that has been codified as "Esoteric Hitlerism," wrote of Hitler as the Man against Time in *The Lightning and the Sun*. Hitler as avatar of the Hindu God Vishnu is something that will not truck with anyone other than the over-literate handful who get lost somewhere between the weeds of irony and the forests of sincerity, but it is impossible not to be drawn into this concept of Hitler as the Man against Time.

According to Devi's work, Men in Time are the Lightning, the destructive energies of civilizational conflict that keep the world in cyclical decay. Men above Time are the Sun, the creative and life-affirming qualities that elevate civilization above decay and create the renewal that can usher in golden ages. The Men against Time, however, are the Lightning and the Sun, combining both of these qualities in order to create a new order and golden age of the Sun through the destructive and leveling qualities of the Lightning. To give birth to life you must also sweep away the dead.

Devi writes in *The Lightning and the Sun*:

> And in an epoch such as that in which we are now living—when, all over the world, every possible attempt is made to present him not merely as "a war monger" but as the "war criminal" number one,—it is not superfluous to stress the fact that Adolf Hitler was, not only at the dawn of his awakening as a "Man against Time" but all his life, "a bitter enemy of war" as such; the fact that he

was by nature "gifted with deep sensitiveness, and full of sympathy for others;" that his programme was essentially a constructive one, his struggle, the struggle for an exalted, positive aim, his aim: the regeneration of higher mankind (of the only section of mankind worth saving) and, ultimately, through the survival of regenerated higher mankind, the restoration of the long-destroyed harmony between the cosmic Order and the sociopolitical conditions on earth, i.e., the restoration of Golden Age conditions; the opening not merely of a "new era" for Germany, but of a new Time-cycle for the whole world.

Many will quibble with Devi's effusive views of Hitler. Many will balk at this oracular perspective. None can deny however that Hitler has a particular quality to him that defies description and so anyone willing to broach this forbidden subject soon discovers that Hitler becomes not just a mirror to the person who approaches his subject, but a magnifier of everything that pours out of them. That same effusive view of Hitler as "a bitter enemy of war" or as a "Man of Peace" would get another writer in trouble: Wyndham Lewis in his 1931 treatise *Hitler*.

This is the quality that Wyndham Lewis wished to capture in his analysis of Hitler. He knew there was something there, but he also knew how unhappy his English audience would be at his attempt to uncover the mystery of the "Hitlerites" without screaming "demons!" at every explanation of their growing movement. The English language is replete with thought-terminating clichés like "it is what it is," signifying that things may just happen for no reason and have no explanation. "But of course an entire country could fall under the hypnotic spell of the man with the magical mustache who could lie bald-faced to them, lie big, and make them do things that are simply against their better nature! It just happens!" Lewis understood this sentiment was bunk and wanted to understand what was really going on, no matter how offended his audience would be at the National Socialist views on everything, but especially economics and Jews.

FOREWORD

Wyndham Lewis is not a figure you'll hear about much except from people who really like Wyndham Lewis. He was both a painter and a writer, though he is probably more known these days for his writings than his paintings. Lewis was in many ways the embodiment of the pan-Anglo experience of the expansive and fungible global empire. Born to an English mother and an American father off the coast of Canada in 1882, in some respects his life superficially paralleled his future subject Adolf Hitler and made him an effective counterpart. Both men had difficult family lives with disappointed fathers; Hitler's beat him while Lewis' wrote to his estranged wife: "Am greatly disappointed with the boy and have unpleasant misgivings about his future." Both men lived in the gray zones of what their nations were, with Lewis' pan-Anglo identity and Hitler's experience of being an Austrian with a German Bavarian dialect putting him in a world without inner Teutonic borders. Both men served heroically in the Great War and both men were artists constantly on the outs of society. Both men inevitably were drawn to fascism with a small f but sought to find their own way. Lewis however is rarely connected with Adolf Hitler except in his explicit work he wrote on him, a "shame" that would dog him for the rest of his life and would be frequently ignored by his admirers who want to admire him on his own terms. But writing *Hitler* would leave its own undeniable mark. His own scarlet A, as it were.

Prior to writing *Hitler*, much of Lewis' life followed that early fascist track. The explosive energy that informed many of the modernist and avant-garde movements that informed early fascism, as those young men were not reactionaries but a new type of man dissatisfied with liberal bourgeois society, was found within Wyndham Lewis as well. He started his own aesthetic movement called "Vorticism," an Anglo alternative to the Expressionist, Cubist, and Futurist movements that had lit an artistic flame in continental Europe and were often hand-in-hand with radical politics; many of the first Fascists in Italy had risen

FOREWORD

up out of Futurism. Perhaps because England had more to look back on, and less to look forward to watching their sun just beginning to set, Lewis's work never quite made the same cultural, but especially political, impact as the Futurists.

Starting first as a painter, he would begin his writing career with the modernist novel *Tarr*, a typical novel about the frustrations of artistic young men angry at phonies and poseurs with money who fashion themselves bohemians. More parallels between the lives of Hitler and Lewis can be found in this novel as the two main characters are the Englishman Tarr, a ready stand-in for Wyndham Lewis, and the German Otto Kreisler, an angry failed artist brimming with explosive creative energy and whose desire to protect his honor leads to him killing a Pole in a duel and then committing suicide before he can be properly brought to justice.

Through the 1920s Lewis would throw himself into the role of the constant satirist of the people and world he knew and positioned himself as their perpetual enemy, declaring himself as such by launching a magazine entitled *The Enemy*. There was philosophy in his writings and critiques however and he sought to find a more perfect Western world in works such as *The Art of Being Ruled* and *Time and Western Man*. At the close of the decade he would write a brutal satire of the London literary world entitled *The Apes of God* which would have been enough to keep him on the outs of "respectable" cultural elites were it not for what he would publish next.

While Lewis brawled with the intelligentsia in the Anglo world in the 1920s, Hitler and the National Socialist German Workers Party brawled in the streets and at the polls of Germany's deeply divided Weimar Republic. Hitler and the NSDAP did not suddenly sneak up on the world; there were enough outside observers that were aware and raised various levels of alarm at their presence as the National Socialist fortunes waxed and waned. While the 1933 elections were the bolt from the brown that caused the whole world to rub their sleepy eyes and take notice of what was going on, Wyndham Lewis just happened to be in Germany during the National Socialists' meteoric 1930 rise: the May 1928 election had given them 2.6 percent of the vote while the September 1930 election netted them 18.3 percent and the second largest number of seats in the Reichstag. The Nazis had arrived under the linden trees, and Lewis was there in the midst of Babylon Berlin.

He had actually only arrived in Germany in November of 1930, two months after the earth-shattering election. His initial reason for arrival had been to seek a German publisher for *The Apes of God*, a curious mission given the limited appeal that a satire on London literary figures would have certainly had on a German public in the midst of their own deep culture war. While on this trip he got to experience first-hand this National Socialist movement that was sending shivers down the spine of European leaders. He was certainly fascinated—how could he not be—and hatched what he thought would be a lucrative journalistic scheme: an English-language profile and explanation of this movement and its enigmatic leader Adolf Hitler. He dashed off forty thousand words on the subject, titled it *Hitler*, and sent it for publishing within months of his stay in Germany.

Lewis received only a one hundred pound advance for this timely work—sixty-eight hundred pounds today or eighty-eight hundred US dollars. For someone as well known and established as Wyndham Lewis, this was the equivalent of a first-time and unknown author getting their first advance. That was as much as the publisher would offer even after Lewis insisted on its worth and topicality. Pennies on the dollar.

The book permanently damaged Lewis' work, but it did not bury him. Ironically what saved him was likely being so early with it, allowing him to claim being duped or foolish when it came time for international liberalism to wipe the slate clean. It was still a rather large brick that Lewis added to his own mausoleum, even if antagonizing the culturally powerful and being associated with men like Ezra Pound, while preferring the Black principle (Fascists) over the Red one (Bolsheviks), built that foundation.

While *Hitler* by Wyndham Lewis is as forgotten as the man himself is unforgotten, it has the honor of being the first book to study the phenomenon of Hitler and the National Socialists. Its value as a literary artifact of a time is unmistakable. First impressions are always the most fascinating and you won't find a work as nuanced, right and wrong, and complex as this work. Time capsules are so few and far between and are especially ignored by historians who require a unified picture of the past. Thus Lewis' work occupies a curious and similar space as Kerry Thornley's *The Idle Warriors*, the only work to have profiled Lee Harvey Oswald *before* the Kennedy assassination.

There is some amusement in the contemporary reaction to the work. The liberal and left-wing reaction is boring and predictable with the same kind of tut-tutting, screeching, and kvetching, while the right-wing reaction is much more interesting. *Some Sort of Genius* by Paul O'Keeffe asserts that "the Honorary Secretary of the Kensington Fascist group took issue with Lewis's assertion that Germany was a far greater nation than Italy," for example. *Some Sort of Genius* sheds further light on why this work is largely unknown to this day as "it was criticized for being biased, sloppily written, badly researched and inaccurate. But nowhere was it condemned as morally tainted. Supporting Fascism or National Socialism did not carry with it the stigma in 1931 that it would carry two years later."

Wyndham Lewis' account of Hitler and the events and environment that precipitated his rise may appear like gazing into a funhouse mirror into the past—or a regular mirror after being born and raised in a funhouse. Germany of the early '30s is both alien to our popular imagination but all too familiar in ways that are forbidden to know. Lewis reflected on that German experience first-hand, bringing the public a man-at-the-scene account of the

FOREWORD

decadent Weimar experience that has been fodder for the rule-stick on how far the United States and European nations have come. His account of the Eldorado night club is especially vibrant and diverse.

Eldorado had been the gold standard for "anything goes." It was the pioneer of drug-soaked unisex androgyny, where if one inquired to whatever the dancer was, according to *Voluptuous Panic* by Mel Gordon, the reply was "I am whatever sex you wish me to be, Madame." Marlene Dietrich found a home there before being scooped up into American film while homosexual and possible dabbler in amateur spy-craft Christopher Isherwood was a frequent customer; his experiences would inspire *Cabaret*. Wyndham Lewis writes of Berlin's Eldorado as the "Pervert's Paradise" and vividly of the dancers with the painted red rosette nipples beneath the "male-token of the chin stubble." Eldorado however is just one establishment out of one-hundred and sixty according to Lewis.

Voluptuous Panic provides lurid details of this scene that has become legendary to the discourse surrounding the rise of Hitler and the National Socialists. Gordon quotes from the Italian journalist and politician Luigi Barzini in his 1983 memoir *The Europeans* on just what sort of delights were available to those willing to seek them within Babylon Berlin:

> I saw pimps offering anything to anybody, little boys, little girls, robust young men, libidinous women, animals. The story went around that a male goose of which one cut the neck at the ecstatic moment would give you the most delicious, economical, and time-saving frisson of all, as it allowed you to enjoy sodomy, bestiality, homosexuality, necrophilia and sadism at one stroke. Gastronomy too, as one could eat the goose afterwards.

While many focus on the apocryphal goose story, there was no doubt much to gander at in this night scene to the point that the name Weimar itself has become a synonym for the lowest reaches of hedonism. It is no wonder then that, according to Lewis in *Hitler*, that:

> Sooner or later [the National Socialist] would desire to be at the head, or in the midst, of his *Sturmabteilung*—to roll this nigger-dance luxury-spot up like a verminous carpet, and drop it into the Spree. (pg. 19)

This was the moment that Lewis wished to capture. Everyone seemed to know that something historical and revolutionary was happening, that the smell of it was in the air for everyone to breathe. And no matter how much Lewis wanted to be the neutral observer of this rising National Socialist revolution, he could not help but write in wonder of it in the same way that would-be nationalists and dissidents within the dominating liberal hegemony would look back on it for inspiration.

Dominique Venner reflecting on the National Socialist revolution in *For a Positive Critique* saw it as nothing the next wave of nationalists could emulate. It wasn't a recipe you could just replicate: add one Weimar Republic, two dashes of degenerate culture, mix with street violence, bake in anger until ready. The times had changed, the tactics were now wrong. What had greatly frightened many who saw the rise of the National Socialists were their revolutionary progressive nature. And Lewis notes this in *Hitler*. These were not the staid conservatives and reactionaries that could be battered around like the straw-men they volunteered themselves to be, but a rejuvenating force that sought to capture the spirit of the times and master it to their own will by hook or by crook. Lewis saw in Hitler at the time the oneness that was so lacking in nationalist reactions. He compares Hitler to the French integralist Charles Maurras who may have been an aristocrat of the soul but lacked the Everyman touch that Hitler seemed to embody. Hitler's critics from the right are quick to pounce on these vulgar energies though many have missed the irony that Hitler could quite easily have been called the moderate Nazi.

There are passages within *Hitler* that will bring to mind the idea that all of this has happened before and will happen again. Lewis notes the hand-wringing about the energy and minds of the youth being captured by the National Socialists, decades before the word "brainwashed" would enter the lexicon. He notes the hypocrisy that if these young men were Marxists they would be praised but as National Socialists they are suddenly exploited and tricked. The utopian always believes himself to be in the last age, from the liberals to the Marxists to the neoconservatives and to the technological fascists. They may or may not believe that history is written by the victors but they certainly believe that history ends with them. The cycle of history and civilization has been mastered and conquered for all time. They are then promptly buried into nice little dirt plots and the eternal struggle resumes without their consent or permission.

A good portion of the book is taken up by Lewis explaining the concept of *Blutsgefühl*, or blood-feeling. He preemptively dismisses the Anglo and American ability to truly understand what this means. Lewis certainly seems to be aware that his contemporary D.H. Lawrence, who was married to a German woman, had some understanding of this, however. Lawrence, who died in 1930, had coined the term "blood-consciousness" to describe his own sense of essence. Where Lawrence's definition only kept an implication of race however, the German word as Lewis describes it exudes it. Curiously, this word does not appear much outside of a Wyndham Lewis context. There is no etymology to Lawrence's coining of his own English version, but that he was married to Frieda, born Emma Maria Frieda Johanna Freiin von Richthofen, until his dying day raises eyebrows at this coincidence.

There is value in contrasting these two feelings. Lewis describes *Blutsgefühl* as the foundation of National Socialism and as "a closer and closer drawing together of the people of one race and culture, by means of bodily attraction...a true bodily solidarity." Lawrence in his description of "blood-consciousness" was reacting to the popularity of Freudian psychoanalysis in his day and offered an alternative understanding in *Fantasia of the Unconscious:*

> Sex is our deepest form of consciousness. It is utterly non-ideal, non-mental. It is pure blood-consciousness. It is the basic consciousness of the blood, the nearest thing in us to pure material consciousness. It is the consciousness of the night, when the soul is almost asleep. The blood-consciousness is the first and last knowledge of the living soul: the depths. It is the soul acting in part only, speaking with its first hoarse half-voice.

For Lawrence there was a becoming of man in the blood-consciousness. For Lewis, he understood *Blutsgefühl* as the becoming of race in feeling. Both currents were in one form or another the emergence of essence. Become who you are, as the cliché goes. For Wyndham Lewis, however, there must be a rejection of the "exotic sense," something he saw D.H. Lawrence and other writers indulging in. Per Lewis: *"What after all is the exoticist, but the White conqueror turned literary and sentimental?"* (pg. 75)

Lewis is a bit harsh on Lawrence in his explanation of the exotic sense, though sensing rightly that Lawrence had too much sympathy for the "renegades" against Western Civilization even if he exhorted his readers that they could not go to the savages. There was something within England (as well as France) that Lewis notes tended toward fascination, sympathy, and engaging the exotic. Orientalism was strongest in both England and France, coupled in England's case with feelings of Zionism (and not coincidentally frequent pederasty), but there was also some affection for the Sub-Saharan African, both in culture (especially

FOREWORD

in its Americanized form) and as a tool in the racial subjugation of European enemies.

Simms in *Hitler: A Global Biography* argues that Hitler was obsessed more with the Anglo nations of Britain and the United States and its international and colonizing financial capitalism than he was with Bolshevik Russia. Detractors to this thesis point to the respect that Hitler had for the British, but this is not necessarily a contradiction. One can have a terrible awe for the power of a rival, and certainly Hitler saw the endgame of history as a great civil war between the emergent Aryan superpowers. Simms backs up his thesis with the shock and awe felt by the Germans at the way the supreme colonial powers had either absorbed German emigrants into their own ranks, turning volkish boys against the fatherland, or the way they deployed a dark rainbow horde from the colonies to sweep against the Central Power within European land. France in particular was known for its vindictiveness with which it deployed Senegalese soldiers to kill and then to police the Rhineland as a form of biopower and racial warfare. Though historians downplay the number of mixed race "Rhineland bastards" that were born from the African soldiers stationed in the Rhineland, the effect of it was enough that it became one of the most prominent rallying tools for the National Socialists.

The big lie of this era is that modern men thought and behaved like postmodern men, that segregationists who stormed the beaches of Normandy did so because they were proto-Antifa. The big lie of this era is that race belief was even then the realm of cranks, or that it was so fully discredited by argument that race-thought was never thought of again. This despite *The Rising Tide of Color Against White World-Supremacy* by Lothrop Stoddard being important enough to be referenced in *The Great Gatsby* and H.G. Wells painting a world where European men are policed and beaten by black policemen in their own cities in the dystopian novel *The Sleeper Awakes*. In his 1936 novel *Absalom, Absalom!*,

FOREWORD

William Faulkner's Canadian character Shreve turns into a terrible seer about the mixed-race descendants of terrible white men swarming the earth:

> I think that in time the Jim Bonds are going to conquer the western hemisphere. Of course it won't quite be in our time and of course as they spread toward the poles they will bleach out again like the rabbits and the birds do, so they won't show up so sharp against the snow. But it will still be Jim Bond; and so in a few thousand years, I who regard you will also have sprung from the loins of African kings.

Within the chapter "The Fox and the Goose," Lewis reveals much more of his intentions and his heart. A thoughtful veteran of the Great War, he knew its innumerable questions went unresolved. And like Enoch Powell he saw a deluge of blood in the river that was rising. He constantly cautions, hedging his bets, knowing it will never be safe for him to say that Hitler has some good answers to some good questions, and so he all but endorses the "Hitlerist" position as he praises Hitler's understanding of the struggle ahead.

For Lewis this is the struggle against extinction. Perhaps as an Englishman he knew there would be no true resistance from the Empire to its conquered subjects returning home to roost. It was fitting that he would see this in animal terms as the Aryans are endangered and have been since Lewis wrote his book. It is undeniable when people like tiny Tim Wise make statements such as:

> In the pantheon of American history, conservative old white people have pretty much always been the bad guys, the keepers of the hegemonic and reactionary flame, the folks unwilling to share the category of American with others on equal terms. Fine, keep it up. It doesn't matter. Because you're on the endangered list. And unlike, say, the bald eagle or some exotic species of muskrat, you are not worth saving.

FOREWORD

These are not the only familiar feelings to be found within Wyndham Lewis' *Hitler*. The reader will find that as they are transported back to the 1930s in Lewis' writing just how little has actually changed in the discourse. The same discourses over what is white and Aryan and what about the high IQ of Ashkenazi Jews like Albert Einstein, that the idea of nation is a little absurd because it was a recent construction and these nations are more provincial and tribal than you assert, and does that not shake your confidence in your beliefs are all to be found in these writings. The non-liberal, of course, must answer ten thousand volleys to their beliefs while the project of liberal supremacy, which often withers at the merest objections made by men like Carl Schmitt, is protected from a single one. That is the struggle though, is it not? Hegemony is its own morality, especially the hegemon that fancies itself the most supreme for being kinder, gentler, and more inclusive.

Despite these nuances, this is a book that is unlikely to change many minds or opinions on Hitler. Its great value is as a curiosity of its time, though not for the reasons one would expect. There are no revelatory insights into Hitler or the "Hitler movement." What the reader may find themselves asking over and over again is "why did Lewis write this when he had no expectation of changing English minds?" The work is suffused with a pessimistic tone toward the English people in their ability to understand who the National Socialists were and why they were as they were. Chapters are spent explaining just why the English will not be able to understand.

The 1930s were a turbulent decade for Lewis, especially politically. He ran into the position many of those who were anti-communist found themselves in: that you might have to take a stand against communism alongside people your enemies really hate. In *Count Your Dead*, Lewis opined on the Spanish Civil War and found himself predictably in the minority of English intelligentsia when he called Franco:

FOREWORD

No more a Fascist than you are, but a Catholic soldier who didn't like seeing priests and nuns killed...didn't want to see all his friends murdered for no better reason than that they all went to mass and the more expensive cafes and usually were able to scrape enough money together to have a haircut and a shave.

Lewis found himself stuck in a position all too familiar to right-wingers in the Anglo sphere: what to do when the choices are a left-wing who provide one terrible choice and conservatives who offer nothing at all. Six years earlier in *Hitler* these same sentiments were there when Lewis wrote:

So, even if Hitlerism, in its pure "Germanism," might retain too much personality, of a second-rate order, nevertheless Hitlerism seems preferable to Communism, which would have none at all, if it had its way. (pg. 119)

This initial book by Lewis comes from the tradition of Anglo empiricism along the veins of Lothrop Stoddard, A.J.P. Taylor, David Irving, and Henry Ashby Turner. Lewis was the quintessential progressive artist and his draw to Hitlerism is as much novelty-seeking as much as it was sympathy for the devil, the ultimate underdog. In 1930 the opposition to the National Socialists had reached a fever pitch. The Social Democrats were firmly in control of Prussia and its police force and used every opportunity to harass and prosecute the National Socialists in a manner that would be familiar to political dissidents today. Lewis was never forgiven for cataloging this in *Hitler* and the portrayal has been thrown into the piles of "bias" and "historical misrepresentation" even as he lived and saw the history himself.

The murder of Horst Wessel by a Communist street pimp, led to Wessel's door by his Communist landlord, put an exclamation mark on the violence of that era. Violence which would only intensify when the KPD (Communist Party of German) began an open campaign of assassination against pro-NSDAP bar owners in the autumn of the next year. Despite living through this history, Lewis was to later rue his romanticization of the NSDAP's early struggles.

What would cause a man who once wrote in *Hitler* "When *two nations* fall out, the armament-king and chemical-king rake in the shekels. When two men fall out, the lawyer coins money. When two *classes* fall out, it is the same thing. Power, or wealth, passes from both to some *third* class" (pg. 49) to disavow Adolf Hitler and take up the cause of the poor downtrodden Jew? It was not the fact that the NSDAP was no longer novel or the underdog, or they failed to uphold campaign promises. Rather Lewis changed his tone because the persecution he observed in Germany was finally brought to bear on him.

He ran and he ran hard. He ran from his own work as he was no William Joyce, a man with whom he had also briefly associated but who was willing to throw all in with the Germans, who at his trumped-up execution stated "I am proud to die for my ideals and I am sorry for the sons of Britain who have died without knowing why." He was known to have visited the leader of the British Union of Fascists, Oswald Mosley, who reflected on him in his autobiography as a man who "used to come to see [him] in most conspiratorial fashion, at dead of night with his coat collar turned up." Wherever and whenever Lewis was asked about the Hitler book after the rise of the National Socialists he was happy to let it be pulped. "And pulp it accordingly became," he wrote.

Even before the situation with his connections to Ezra Pound and whispers of treason made him try to expunge any all memories of that turbulent period, he attempted to rectify his position and weather the coming storm. He worked hard to absolve himself by 1939 as the next European war was increasingly inevitable, publishing in that same year two works meant to give him the plausible deniability from his past that he desperately sought. The first was the complete repudiation of *Hitler* entitled *The Hitler Cult* and the second a satire on anti-Semitism entitled *The Jews,*

FOREWORD

Are They Human?

Even within *The Hitler Cult*, Lewis finds the necessity to invent Hitler. He recites his litany of experiences with the National Socialists in order to show that his contact with them was quite limited. The parallel prophetic powers of Lewis continue within this work—just as he foresaw the beginning of a Hitler in *Tarr*, he saw his incoming end six years later in *The Hitler Cult*:

> National Socialism will die a violent death: everything points to that solution. I give it a few years at the outside. It may die in battle: it may blow its brains out: it may burst: it may merge insensibly into something else. But it will no longer be there in, let us say, six years' time. I should be sorry to assert that all those who execrate it are saints, or even honest men. But from whatever angle you observe it, it is not an attractive phenomenon. Hardly an intelligent man will be found who will regret it.

Meanwhile in *The Jews, Are They Human?* Lewis throws himself at the feet of philosemitism, an easy task for an Englishman. Even within *Hitler* Lewis was walking the edges of it, reminding his English audience just how much they had civilized the Jewish people and entered into harmonious matrimony with them. He continues this track in *The Jews, Are They Human?*, writing obsequious passages to the Jews that were no doubt meant to chase off the audience that he feared he had cultivated. Lewis was a satirical writer who bit whom he could until he could draw the piss out of them, but *The Jews, Are They Human?* is so craven in its self-deprecatory humor one can't help but think of a beaten dog scuttering around its master. Take for example this passage on the relationship between the Jews and the English:

> Then, even if they did decide to remain with us, the Jews are one of the most industrious races in the world; and we are one of the least industrious. They will set a high standard of hard work at least, which it will be necessary for the rest of us to live up to.

FOREWORD

That will be most salutary. It is worth paying people to come here to teach us how to work! We could not have better instructors.

Through the 1940s, Lewis tried to get himself back into the good graces of liberal society by praising men like Franklin Delano Roosevelt and the melting pot and the racial incoherency of the United States. Memories were longer than Lewis wished to give people credit for, and his brief star never shone brightly ever again. By the early 1950s Lewis was blind and beginning his slow shuffle into his 1957 grave. Those memories of his flirtation with fascism lasted long enough that after he had made enemies of all the earth more than enough of them were quite willing to let him be forgotten, and for much of literary history, he was. The man that W.H. Auden once called "that lonely old volcano of the Right" sputtered off into obscurity and became less of a volcano and more of a fire anthill.

Nearly ninety years since *Hitler* was first published one comes away thinking that Lewis had given up before the fighting even started. The English are as they are and they're never going to change. There'll always be an England, as the famous song went. But will there be? Vera Lynn has only passed away in this *Anno Domini* of 2020. One wonders what she thought looking around living through the years since Lewis published *Hitler* and the changes England underwent until the day she died.

While Wyndham Lewis retains a small cadre of devoted followers, largely Anglophiles, students of modernism, and fans of the era, it is certain that interest in him will rise in conjunction with interest in his work on Adolf Hitler. The men lived parallel lives and Lewis being the elder brother thought he could keep a step ahead of the little brother and his tide. *Hitler* was pulped, its ideas supposedly supplanted in subsequent works and yet here it is almost a century later. Literary immortality, whether Lewis liked it or not.

Hitler is not going anywhere. This is his world and we're all just living in it, whether his followers win or fail. As the philosopher Søren Kierkegaard scribbled down in his journals, "The tyrant dies and his rule is over, the martyr dies and his rule begins."

In Hitler's case, it might be said to be both.

PART I

BERLIN

THE WEIMAR REPUBLIC AND THE *DRITTE REICH*

Writing in the *Saturday Review* of December 13th, 1930, Dr. Benes commenced his article as follows:

> Germany holds the key of the New Europe. What happens there within the next few months will decide the course of European politics for years to come. Geographically in the center of the Continent, Germany is the political and the economic hub of Europe. It is in this country that 7,000,000 citizens have just voted to put into power a movement which promised to tear up the treaties which are the basis of the European settlement and the foundation of the League of Nations.

That movement is the *Hitler Bewegung*, the so-called National Socialism that is the creation of Adolf Hitler. It is, I am persuaded, a phenomenon that deserves a great deal of attention. It might very well be a deciding factor in the political world—for Germany, besides being "the political and the economic hub of Europe," is, as well, a very great country, and what it dreams and wishes and resents cannot be lightly set aside.

In the following articles it is as an exponent—not as critic nor yet as advocate—of German National Socialism, or Hitlerism, that I come forward. It seems to me very important that an unprejudiced and fairly detailed account of this great and novel factor in world affairs should be at the disposal of the intelligent Anglo-Saxon. The Anglo-Saxon reader will violently dissent from many of the views and attitudes of the Hitlerite. The latter's economic policy will appear at first sight mad, his attitude to the Jewish people almost incomprehensible. But I shall not present the National Socialist standpoint in general in an unreal manner calculated to appeal to and mislead the Englishman or the American. At the start it is better to display in their full violence and extremism (and extremism of any sort is highly antipathetic to the Anglo-Saxon)—with all their logical consequences unsoftened—these bitter interpretations of current history, these wildly idealistic National Socialism proposals for the "conquest of the Western soul," and for the founding of a peaceful confederacy of "Aryan" states. To the best of my ability, I will outline the financial measures envisaged. However fantastic they may at first sight appear, I suggest that it would be inadvisable to stop the ear and shut the eye immediately against such seemingly insane combinations, effected by means of a fiery fusion of all that is most outrageous to the mind of the sober, tolerant, democratic average, snatched from the armory of the extreme left and of the extreme right.

How I came to have the idea of writing these articles was as follows. I went to Berlin recently on business, and there I spent some weeks. But I found myself at once encompassed by a strange political unrest. Generally inattentive to politics, I found it impossible to escape from these—not so much because I agreed with the matter or the tone of them (indeed, I am exceedingly skeptical about, and unresponsive to, all nationalist excitements whatever), as because there was an unmistakable accent of passion and of impressive conviction in this particular agitation that I had not met with before upon the European scene.

The powerful machine of the methodical German consciousness is able to set up more imposing waves, once it gives its mind to it, than, for instance, the national mind in ebullition of Italy or of Spain. I was in Italy upon the eve of the March on Rome (with *"A Morte Mussolini!"* scribbled in chalk everywhere upon the walls of the venetian houses, and also *"Evviva"*), and in Spain, at the time of the first artillery revolt, for three days obstructed by martial law in a province. But I found this November, in Berlin, the massive politics of the Reich, and the no less massive and bitter dreams of the *Dritte Reich*, more insistent in their appeal. At first casually, and then more carefully, I found myself observing these grand-scale political maneuvers. These notes are the result.

When, in the winter evenings, along the boulevards of *Berlin im Licht*, the muffled, uniformed hawkers take up their stations and utter their dismal cries, it is not sport, as with us, but politics, that is the dominant motive. Indeed, dismalest and loudest, the *"Nacht Ausgabe"* resounds above the rest; and *that* is the organ of Hugenberg; and if you buy it you will find it packed, beneath huge type, with the accounts of the latest dirty trick played by Herr Grzesinski, the police president of Berlin, upon the National Socialists (who are the close allies of Hugenberg), or the latest student riot, occurring in response to the latest oppressive measure dictated by the Social-democratic, or Prussian Socialist, authorities, to the detriment of the academic youth. The cry of *"Tempo"* is lighter than that of the *"Nacht Ausgabe"*; but buying that, you will immediately learn from the masters of *Tempo* that those of the *Nacht Ausgabe* are terribly in the wrong, and as un-patriotic as you had just learned the masters of *Tempo* to be. And those people who read the *Tempo* look askance at those who read the *Nacht Ausgabe*—adherents respectively of the Weimar Republic and of the *Dritte Reich*.

In a general way, it may be said that the patriotism of the latter asserts that all truly patriotic Germans will refuse to pay their war debts, whereas the former vociferates that all true German patriots will applaud those politicians who tax them afresh every day, so that Germany, in this way "bled white," may satisfy its creditors. It is easy to imagine which of these two theories has the most immediate patriotic appeal. The appeal to the purse is all upon the side of Hugenberg; and as to pure Germanhood, there again the *Bankleute* of the *Erfühlungspolitik* are not so German as he, or so it is said.

The *Nationalsozialistische Deutsche Arbeiter Partei*, then, is the creation of, and largely depends upon, one man, that is Adolf Hitler, who is an Austrian house-painter, just over forty years old. He served in a Bavarian regiment during the War with distinction:

now he is the leader of a party of 107 deputies in the Reichstag but is himself disqualified from sitting in the German parliament, because he is not a German citizen. But the Hitler movement, at the moment of its great victory at the polls in September last, received so much advertisement in the English press that most people, no doubt, are aware of its existence and acquainted with a few of the main features of its program.

Since that time, however, the popular press in England has, for the most part, left it alone. In consequence, the impression exists here that it is snuffed out, and that Hitler is politically extinct. That is, however, not the case—quite the reverse. In municipal elections that took place in different parts of Germany during November (in Baden, Mecklenburg, Danzig, in Bremen, Munich University, etc.) the National Socialists have everywhere enormously increased the number of their votes.

Thus, in Karlsruhe a quarter of the poll in the Reichstag election in September went to Hitler. But in the November municipal elections his followers polled one-third—18,880 votes was the actual figure. The next largest party was the Socialist, with 12,710 votes.

Still more surprising was the National Socialist success in the Bremen elections of November 31st There the Reichstag vote—the September vote—of the National Socialist Party stood at 26,137. But two months later the number of people in Bremen voting National Socialist had increased to 51,324. The Communists even lost a fifth of their votes to the National Socialists. That was particularly significant. Again, the Social Democrats polled 10,000 votes less than in the Reichstag election in September, and 20,000 less than in that of 1927.

These figures will serve to indicate that the state of affairs brought about through the Reichstag election of last September, by the Hitlerist victory, has not passed away in a puff of world-excitement and newspaper scare headlines. It is becoming an established fact in every part of the German Reich.

The Berlin correspondent of the *Observer* wrote (December 7th):

> Something comparable only to a national-religious upheaval has taken deep root in the people's minds.... Adolf Hitler...caused Germany's ex-enemies, her present creditors, to sit up and take notice. He gained more publicity for his views abroad in as many days than the Nationalists of the old school in as many years.

In the phrase, "Nationalists of the old school," you have, perhaps, the gist of the matter—Hitler is a very new type of nationalist in Germany. The people who follow him know that the Junker spirit plays no part in his eloquent workman's evangel. And even more remarkable than that, the specifically Russian (the Hitlerites, of course, would say Jewish-Russian) social-religion, Marxism or communism, also plays no part. He has with him Hohenzollern princes, but also he has the converted communist, Otto Strasser (the title of a pamphlet, *Der Sowjetstern geht unter*, indicates clearly the attitude of this ex-Marxist). And any average National Socialist *Sturmabteilung* is made up of young men—who, were it not for the superior allurement of this religion of Hitler's—with its banners, its military discipline, its elevated idealism and dreams of a *Dritte Reich*, its martyrdoms, its "Horst Wessel Song"—would be equally fanatical adepts of the religion of Moscow and of Marx.

The other day I was present at a monster meeting of National Socialists at the *Sportpalast*, in Berlin. Goebbels and Göring (a flying ace during the War, and now a Hitlerist deputy) were speaking. Here, indeed, was the genuine atmosphere of national-religious upheaval of which the correspondent of the *Observer* speaks. In this gigantic assembly of twenty thousand people there was something like the physical pressure of one immense, indignant thought—it was impossible to be present and not to be amazed at the passion engendered in all these men and women, and the millions of others of whom these were only a fraction, by the message of these stormy platform voices, calling upon them to pursue relentlessly the path marked out, and to recapture their freedom at whatever cost. Goebbels (unique as organizer and at the same time revolutionary agitator—not such a common combination) was a tiny, nervous figure, whose voice rose constantly to a scream, as he denounced the present misrule—the tribute-politics, *Erfühlungspolitik*—the terroristic methods—the stream of taxation, the credit monopolies of the Social-democratic, and now the Centre Coalition, ruling dictatorially by presidential decree—of Brüning and of Severing, and their *Erfühlungskabinett*.

BERLIN *IM LICHT*
———◆———

In order to understand the nature of the political cinema unrolling itself in the German capital, with many a hefty start and flick, the foreigner should somehow get a good physical picture of the aspect of the place where all these vigorous events take place, and prop it up before him so that he may be present to it as he reads. That is essential.

Berlin is, of course, a very large and relatively new city, laid out upon ample imperial lines. But whereas ten years ago the social center of the city was in the district of *Unter den Linden*, that part of Berlin has now become the business quarter. It is the center, as well, of academic life: the University is there.

The dazzling boulevard-world of *Berlin Westens*, that is where to look for the social centers—there are to be found the arteries where money flows. It would not be true to say that Rank and Fashion have moved there. This huge gimcrack West End of the luxury night-life wonder-town—resembling after dark nothing so much as Broadway and its neighborhood at the same hour—is a brand-new contraption.

It is the bedizened fortress of the *Schiebertum*. It has *moved* from nowhere—horizontally. It is mostly a stark jack-in-the-box underworld popped up, with a prodigious clatter, and there it stands, as pleased as Punch. The name "Kempinski" would be first key to the secret of its uprush. Kempinski and a fair, false *Deutschtum*.

Berlin Westens and all it means was thrown up by the War out of the Earth's bowels, as it were, from sweated cellars, traps, and gutters. It established itself overnight in the Kurfürsten-damm, Nollendorf Platz, Wittenberg Platz, Motzestrasse, Tauenzien-strasse, and so forth, far away from the old centers of imperial life, whose empty palaces, and also rather empty shops, have been left more or less derelict.

The final touch came about two years ago. It is the electrical drumfire, the high-volted light-bombardment from all sides, that is the finishing stroke. A great campaign, with the popular label *Berlin im Licht!* was inaugurated by the *Asphaltpresse*—that was somewhere in 1928, I think. The spurious Germanism of the colossal Wagnerian *Vaterland* of Kempinski, along with a thousand other night-circuses, Negertanz palaces, *naktballeten*, *flagellation-bars*, and sad wells of super-masculine loneliness, shining dives for the sleek stock-jobbing sleuth relaxing, and so forth, did indeed most luridly light themselves up and flaunt their names in fashionable electricity, to such good effect that, although Berlin cannot emulate the perpendicular night-scenery of the wan canons and search-lit altitudes of New York City, it yet does decidedly convey an air of heavy and louche brilliance, as of a really first-class *mauvais lieu*. No city has anything on it as regards the stark suggestions of being the Hauptstadt of Vice, the excelsior Eldorado of a sexish bottom-wagging most arch Old Nick sunk in a costly and succulent rut—and that is what Berlin wanted, if by Berlin is meant that gilt-edged limelit fraction that enjoys *Berlin im Licht*.

Paris has nothing to show at all like *Berlin Westens*. New York under prohibition is a poor place in comparison. Only drinking wood-alcohol and bad Chianti in luxurious cellars and gilded slums, New York lacks, as a public place, the liquorous amenities of a "fallen" world, best symbolized perhaps by such resorts as "Eldorado"—the Eldorado of the Motzestrasse (there are two).

In harmony with all this, gang-violence in Berlin abounds, the armed *Zuhälter* or pimp fattens and flourishes. Berlin can show what is probably the most oddly unlovely gunmen of the Earth. The Berlin correspondent of the *Daily Express* remarked the other day (December 15th, 1930) in the course of a description of a night-battle between armed police and three hundred gunmen, that "Berlin... is now assuming the character of a European Chicago."

That this assimilation of Berlin to Chicago is not confined to foreign observers may be seen from the following account from *Der Angriff* (January 15th, 1931)—except that here it is claimed that "the state of affairs in Chicago...is already surpassed":

> ...kommunistische Horden systematisch Tag für Tag und Nacht für Nacht ganze Strassenzüge terrorisieren konnen, wo dauernd Schüsse fallen, Wohnungen gestürmt werden, Nationalsozialisten überfallen, niedergeschlagen, niederschossen werden, und die Polizei dem Treiben dieser roten Verbrecher machtlos gegenübersteht....Eine der schlimmsten Brutstätten des roten Verbrechergesindels ist der Bezirk Kreuzberg. Hier sind die Zustände in Chikago, Amerikas berüchtigter Verbrecherstadt, die wir oft als Beispiel angaben, bereits übertroffen. Hunderte von Kommunisten treiben sich hier schwerbewaffnet auf den Strassen umher...[1]

Yes, Berlin is quite Chicagoan in the matter of the *Untermensch*— but it is something more, far more (as indeed is indicated in the above account). It is, in contrast to the American city, *also*, and *pardessus le marche*, at least *Borgian* in its political temper. No week passes without murderous affrays between the people I am writing about here and the Marxist murder-gangs and armed bravos of other extreme left-wing political sects.

Disorder is rampant and is checked with firearms and *gummiknüppeln*[2] in the streets, and left at that, not suppressed by iron decrees of the supreme authority, as one would expect. The reason for this is not the impotence of the Prussian administration.

---

[1] "...Communist hordes can systematically terrorize whole streets day after day and night, where shots are constantly fired, apartments are stormed, Nazis are attacked, beaten down, shot down, and the police are powerless to the hustle and bustle of these red criminals... One of the worst breeding grounds of the red criminal rabble is the district of Kreuzberg. Here, the conditions in Chicago, America's notorious crime city, which we often used as an example, have already been surpassed. Hundreds of communists are driving around the streets here heavily armed..."

[2] Rubber truncheon.

It is difficult to see what it is, in fact, if it is not the result of a settled policy, or, at all events, of a temper that grudges police defense on behalf of noxious organizations. Street-violence, it could be argued, suits the book of the republican caucus, so at least it would seem. The political opponents of the present republican regime (the most powerful of which are the *Nazis* or National Socialists) can only be held in check by constant police violence. The Communist needs that too. But the Communist helps the police to beat and shoot the Nazis. So (except that the Nazi is disarmed on all occasions and imprisoned for long terms if he is caught in possession of a penknife or pea-shooter) violence all round (when it is not Nazi) is not too absolutely discouraged—at least, so much may, I think, be asserted—by the Republican Government of the Reich. Patrol wagons packed with armed police hurry from spot to spot from dusk to daybreak, bludgeoning, shooting, and arresting: armed bands of one sort and another are usually on the move as well, and more or less seriously clashing.

Boileau, describing Paris in the days of King-Sun, wrote as follows. And the bourgeois-citizen of Berlin, perhaps less wittily exaggerating, could write much the same today of his city:

> Car, sitôt que du soir les ombres pacifiques d'un double cadenas font former les boutiques; que, retiré chex lui, le paisible marchand va revoir ses billets et compter son argent; que dans le Marcheé-Neuf tout est calme et tranquille; les voleurs à l'instant s'emparent de la ville.
>
> Le bois le plus funeste et le moins fréquenté est, au prix de Paris, un lieu de sûreté. Malheur done à celui qu'une affaire impreévue engage un peu trop tard au détour d'une rue! Bientôt quatre bandits lui serrant les côtés: la bourse!... Il faut se rendre; ou bien, non! Résistez!
>
> Afin que votre mort, de tragique mémoire, des massacres fameux aille grossir l'histoire! Pour moi, formant ma porte, et cédant au sommeil, tous les jours je me couche avecque le soleil.
>
> Mais, en ma chambre à peine ai-je éteint la lumière, qu'il ne

m'est plus permis de fermer la paupiere. Des filous effrontés, d'un coup de pistolet, ebranlent ma fenêtre, et percent mon volet. J'entends crier partout: Au meurtre! on m'assassine!

Ou: Le feu vient de prendre à la maison voisinel!³

The "Horst Wessel Song," with which all National Socialist meetings terminate, bears witness to these conditions: for it is the song written by a young Nazi storm-leader, who was shot in his lodgings by a communist gunman, who went there with his band at the request of Wessel's landlady, who desired to be rid of her fascist lodger, whose politics displeased her. But literally thousands of National Socialists have been killed and wounded in affrays, during the last twelve months, in all parts of Germany. Their *Sturmabteilungen* are forever coming up against a *Rollcommando* of the *Reichsbanner*, or falling into a Marxist ambush of the Red-frontfighters. And they have paid this back in kind, Marxist and *Reichsbannerleute* have fallen beneath their daggers and bullets (for sometimes they have been driven to arm).

So, Berlin is Chicago, only more so if anything, but minus bootleg, and with that great difference—that politics account for much of the street violence.

The Marxist gangs take their orders from Moscow instead of

---

³ "Because, as soon as in the evening the peaceful shadows of a double padlock make the shops form; that, withdrawing from him, the peaceful merchant will review his tickets and count his money; that in the Marche-Neuf everything is calm and peaceful; the thieves are taking the city.

The most disastrous and least frequent wood is, at the price of Paris, a place of safety. Woe to him that an unforeseen affair starts a little too late around a street! Soon four bandits clutching his ribs: the purse!...We have to surrender; or not! Resist!

So that your death, tragic memory, famous massacres will go to make history worse! For me, forming my door, and yielding to sleep, every day I go to bed with the sun.

But, in my bedroom, I hardly turned off the light when I was no longer allowed to close my eyelid. Cheeky swindlers, with a pistol, shake my window, and pierce my shutter. I hear shouting everywhere: To murder! they murder me!

Or: The fire has just taken the neighboring house!"

from Capone (Europe is after all no bigger than the States—there is a great deal of coming and going between these capitals). Hitler's is a rival racket. But it is opposite brands of revolution that these guys and mugs traffic in: and as far as the National Socialists are concerned, the pockets of the participants are not lined by any means, or their nests feathered, as a consequence of their dangerous tasks. It is a very disinterested activity. Also, whereas the Communist is invariably armed, the Nazi has only his fists or sticks to defend himself with, owing to the discrimination of the Republican Police Authorities—from the start the Nazis have been incessantly denounced, harassed, and disarmed.

The Nazi Organization further lives under the perpetual threat of a *Verbot*, of suppression throughout Germany. In consequence the Nazi leaders recently have been compelled to issue orders to the effect that any National Socialist discovered in possession of firearms will be expelled from the Party.

So today most of the killing and wounding is done by the other side. Yet in spite of the strict orders to the contrary, it does sometimes happen that Nazis arm themselves, as I have said, in response to extreme provocation, and in face of the certainty of death if they are not in a position to defend themselves: in a small mining town, where they may be comparatively weak in numbers, for instance, or at moments of intensified communist activity. Thus, the brother of Dr. Goebbels (the Berlin leader) is at present in jail with another man for killing a Communist in the course of a clash in a small Rhine town. Goebbels's mother has now been compelled to move to another State because of the repeated threat to her life from local Communists. And there is no part of Germany from which news does not come daily of street-battles. So it is a civil war of sorts that is in progress from the Alps to the North Sea.

The Berlin "Eldorado"

Berlin—its western Babylon—is as everybody knows the *quartier-general* of dogmatic perversity—the Perverts' Paradise, the Mecca of both Lesb and So. I think it argues a great deal of good sense on the part of the National Socialists that they have ignored this feature of the glittering west-end of their city—unlike the young Action Française militants, who some years ago made attacks upon the Paris kiosks, tearing up *La Vie Parisienne* and albums full of Tabarin tarts doing the splits in a cataract of lace.

In point of fact the Berlin kiosks are calculated to enrage the moralist far more than those of Paris. For the nature of the obscene publications for bookstall sale in Berlin would rouse Monsieur Chiappe to a minatory alertness inside of a minute, but apparently leave Herr Grzesinski cold. They also leave the Nazis cold, I am glad to be able to say—they have something better to think about. This seems to me of very great importance in estimating the Nazis. Pink-clothed back-sides are not their political quarry. That is good. The sex-moralist is not only a bore, but should, I think, always be suspect. And then apart from that, "purity" agitations are not only dismally silly, but politically ill-advised. You cannot make war upon an Orbe-Rose, a Rose-Bottom, without making yourself ridiculous.

So the fact that the Nazi is not a sex-moralist at all should be reckoned, I think, as a very good mark indeed, politically and otherwise (I hope that as I write these lines some stupid fanatic or sly traitor in their midst is not stirring them up to lynch some harmless old international lesbian!).

This does not mean to say, however, that the Nazi would regard the public orgasms of the night-life *Bankleute* as edifying. On the contrary. But he would neglect that in order to concentrate upon issues of far more public moment. To put this in a nutshell—*The*

Bank is more important than the Back-side. And the young National Socialist has firmly grasped this fundamental truth, in a manner that no average political Anglo-Saxon would—who always allows his pocket to be picked provided you fix his attention upon something that is "wicked" or naughty. Very sentimental, he always falls in love with what he ought not to do. The political history of England and America in the present age is a long history of astute side-tracking of the great Western democracies down moralist culs-de-sac (*Prohibition* is of course the arch-farce in that direction).

But for us, attempting from afar to establish in the Anglo-Saxon public mind some sort of scientific or informative picture of Berlin (to be a setting for its politics), it is necessary (for us, if not for the Nazi) to take into account all its "Eldorados." Its Eldorados, after all, are within cat's call of its Reichstag. The Hermanstrasse (that is Hitler's Berlin offices) is round the corner from the *Domino Bar*. So I must now for a moment take up the functions of a guide and quickly conduct the Anglo-Saxon reader around a characteristic *Nachtlokal*.

In the Eldorado of the Motzestrasse, first of all, everything is absolutely as it should be in the best of all possible Hollywood cabarets. There is the true appropriate glitter and nigger-hubbub—super-sex and pink champagne. All that is quite regular: all is *comme il faut* as well. No sightseer entering Eldorado, I imagine, would get the frisson of the exotic and the peculiar. Nothing of the sort. Quite the reverse, for all at first sight is depressingly normal. The sightseer might be disappointed even—he might certainly feel that he had been misled into visiting a respectable resort, where nothing naughtier than a simple Victorian strumpet was to be found.

But elegant and usually eyeglassed young women will receive him, with an expensive politeness, and he will buy one of these a drink, and thus become at home. Still, he will have to be a sightseer of some penetration not to think that his sightseeing eyes may not this time be destined to gloat, upon what he had promised them they should find there. Then these bland Junos-gone-wrong, bare-shouldered and braceleted (as statuesque as feminine showgirl guardees), after a drink or two, will whisper to the outlandish sight-seer that they are *men*. Oh dear—so, after all, the sightseeing eyes are going to be satisfied! And they will goggle at the slightly-smiling bland Edwardian "tart" at their side—still disposed to regard this as a hoax after all, for it is too like, it is too true to nature by far.

But his companion will invite the skeptical tourist to pass his disbelieving paw beneath her chin. She will catch hold of it without coyness and ·drag it under this massively fashioned feature. All doubt is then at an end. There, sure enough, the fingers of the sightseer will encounter a bed of harsh unshaven bristles as stiff as those of a tooth-brush.

For six years this very well-behaved and scented man has lived as a woman, the tourist will be told (it is always, for some reason, "six years"). But all these *trompe l'œil*, spurious ladies are so perfectly *normal*, in their manner and the repose with which they prosecute their paradox—they are such perfect imitations—of rather dull, phlegmatic, Swedish, English, or German, tarts (of a somewhat out-moded description)—that still the skeptical sightseer will blink, perhaps. What if after all he is being deceived?

But this will not escape the observant person with whom he is sitting—indeed she has been expecting it. After a short interval it will provoke the gently-smiling, roguish Juno at his side to carry her hands down within the low-cut evening frock, upon the discreet elevation of her breasts: and then her hands will reappear, each holding a wire cup, with cloth stretched over it.

Upon this a red rosette is painted, to represent the nipple. On the other hand, the sightseer will later be importuned to give her hair a pull, to convince himself that it is real—a womanly attribute, to set off the male token of the chin-stubble.

It is more than probable that ever after, in the mind of this average, not very reflective, but dully-questioning mortal, a dull doubt will subsist. The "feminine" will never be quite the same for him again. Who can say if this will be for his good or no? The sex-absolute will to some extent have been disintegrated for him by this brief encounter—it will have caused him to regard, with a certain skeptical squint, all specifically feminine personality. This may, after all (it is perhaps not too venturesome to believe), be of great use to him, even, in the subsequent conduct of his life. Such radical *Enttäuschung* might even be of great economic value to the average sightseer, in his struggle with nature and her expensive traps and tricks.

Of establishments upon these lines, Berlin can boast one hundred and sixty, I believe. Some are the stern strongholds solely of the *lesbische Frau*. There is nothing sunny or pagan about those. All is feverish, solemn, tense—with a furious rictus in place of the bland male smile.

But every variety of perversion is properly and adequately represented. Each has its home-away-from-home, its bar, its club, its bazaar, its place of nightly *Reklame* and rendezvous.

Of course the rough-chinned debutantes, rakish and eye-glassed, are a particular, a most plebeian, type—it is the *Homo vulgus* of the Homosexual Creation. They are very much looked down upon by the more distorted and aristocratic varieties, rather as the Fat Woman may be in a circus, by the more interesting freaks—those with arms growing out of their chests, for instance, or with eyes in their knees (Dame Laura Knight or Lady Eleanor Smith would have to be consulted about this). They are there in the foreground only because these establishments are among the principal showplaces of Berlin, and this "Nancy" conjuring-trick—that of the *trompe l'œil*—is generally found very clever and funny by the average hearty tourist.

But equally for the mere tourist, and for the dispassionate eye of the "restless analyst," these strange women and strange men are "very interestin'," as Van Dine would make Vance say. And the dull naturalism of the male copycat is not to be despised. These pieces of stolid conjuring-trickery have to an astonishing degree the clear and untroubled eyes of very placid village Venuses accustomed to cows and sheep—who see life steadily and see it whole.

But the young German politician, I need hardly remark, does not go to such resorts—for him it would be (morals apart, as I have said—which his pagan health, and the natural Teutonic coarseness and realism, precludes his worrying his head about) out of his line altogether. And of course, all these Bars and Dancings, with their Kaffir bands, are for him the squinting, misbegotten, paradise of the *Schiebertum*. "*Juda verrecke!*" he would no doubt mutter, or shout, if he got into one. Sooner or later he would desire to be at the head, or in the midst, of his *Sturmabteilung*—to roll this nigger-dance luxury-spot up like a verminous carpet, and drop it into the Spree—with a heartfelt *Pfui!* at its big sodden splash. Neither the "restless analyst," nor the guileless tourist, will feel that way about it: that is the attitude of the ascetic of Politics—an asceticism not without its nobility, one that is little understood.

PART II
ADOLF HITLER
THE MAN AND THE PARTY

The Oneness of "Hitlerism" and of Hitler

In setting out to expound the doctrine of Hitlerism, it rapidly becomes apparent that it is rather *a person* than *a doctrine* with which we are dealing. Junius Alter, in his widely-read book upon the German Nationalists of today, remarks, that, as to the National Socialist Party and its leader, "*die beide eine unzertrennliche Einheit bilden,*"[4] Hitlerism is Hitler.

But Adolf Hitler is just a very typical German "man of the people"—"*Mann aus dem Volke,*" just as his movement is a *Volksbewegung*. As even his very appearance suggests, there is nothing whatever eccentric about him. He is not only satisfied with, but enthusiastically embraces, his *typicalness*. So you get in him, cut out in the massive and simple lines of a peasant art, the core of the Teutonic character. And his "doctrine" is essentially just a set of rather primitive laws, promulgated in the interest of that particular stock or type, in order to satisfy its special requirements and ambitions, and to ensure its vigorous survival, intact and true to its racial traditions.

Hitler is *The German Man*—and now he has become a "Man of Destiny" as well. For he is recognized as The German Man by probably fifteen million potential German voters.

So in Adolf Hitler, The German Man, we have, I assert, a "Man of Peace." He is certainly not "a pacifist," of the order of the regulation pacifist best-seller Remarque. But Hitler is as it were the typical German soldier (the *Frontkämpfer* as they a little grandiloquently call it). The Iron Cross, conspicuous upon his bosom, signifies that he is a brave soldier, not that he is a bravo or a pugilist. How should this be otherwise, seeing that he is "a German man of the people?" The *furor teutonicus* has always been

---

[4] "which both form an inseparable unit"

the monopoly of the Prussian noble.

The militant nationalism of the Hitlerist is, again, of a very different order to that much slighter affair, the Action Française nationalism. The latter could fairly be described as amateur nationalism, with something of the erratic effectiveness that that word implies. It is essential to realize too the prodigious organization of the Hitler Movement. And all this huge party-structure is based upon a much more substantial impulse than that animating its puny French counterpart. It is really *national,* in its extent and solidarity, as in the *impersonal* force that it represents. For if this doctrine must be described as a personal one, and if it is necessary continually to be referring back to the individual who gives it his name, Adolf Hitler, yet it is much less personal in fact than the movement inspired by Charles Maurras. Maurras, a great intellectual, aristocratic in temper, is un-typical: whereas Hitler is a sort of inspired and eloquent Everyman.

Hitler is as typical as Mussolini. And the German Nation is greater, *as a nation*, than the Italian—apart from its numerical superiority and vastly more powerful organization: and it must always be infinitely more formidable when acting *as one man.* If Hitler continues to gain ground, as there seems every chance of his doing, Germany will then act *as one man.*

The conjunction of circumstances that have brought all this about—Inflation, Debt, "Young-tribute," Financial Dictatorship, Government by Presidential Decree, supineness of the hereditary princes and all those who ruled Germany prior to the Weimar Republic—that is merely the history of the last, and post-war, decade, which has been a nightmare for this great northern community, already tested beyond endurance by the vast losses and sufferings of the most inhuman and meaningless of all wars.

Everything that is puzzling to the Anglo-Saxon in Hitlerism can be explained if these rudimentary facts are borne in mind. Even the *Judenfrage*—that old man of the sea of the politics of *Mitteleuropa*—if it does not find its justification, finds at least its rationale in this peasant doctrine of fierce exclusiveness, and jealous hard-headed resolve to keep out at all cost the alien, whom the peasant-mind suspects (whether rightly or wrongly—and no doubt sometimes it is one, sometimes the other) of having designs upon its patrimony. We must remember as well that as a result of the inflation this nation of savers found everything they possessed swept away in a torrent of worthless paper money.

Furthermore, there is also the deep animal antipathy to be reckoned with, causing the essential German who is a born provincial to stand upon his guard against a glib metropolitan product, whose ancient and dissimilar culture seems to threaten the integrity of his own traditional ideals.

HITLERISM AND THE *JUDENFRAGE*
―◆―

In the forefront of the Hitlerist Program stand drastic proposals directed against the Jews. As this is calculated in Anglo-Saxon countries to prejudice people at the outset against the movement, that question had better be investigated in some detail at once. In the following pages I will see what I can do with it. It will not, I am afraid, be much, but I hope to soften somewhat the contours of this preliminary snag.

Here it is not part of my task, nor should I care to undertake it, to go into the ins and outs of the *Judenfrage*. As an independent and powerful, and very exclusive, religious community, the Jewish People cannot but be subject to suspicious speculation from time to time, wherever they are established. But, in addition to that, there is of course still in Germany a stark racial distinction which has no counterpart in England. In *Mitteleuropa* there are *Juden* and *Nichtjuden*, here that is not the case.

When Mussolini was asked what he thought about the national Socialist attitude with regard to the "Jewish question," he replied quite sincerely at once, "We have no 'Jewish question' in Italy." An English leader of the same order would reply in exactly the same way: "Never heard of it!" he would snap. "No 'Jewish question' in England, my dear sir! What is a Jewish question, anyway?"

In America there is a Jewish question of sorts, no doubt, but not much. The anti-Semitism that does exist is sustained solely by the extremely bad manners and barbaric aggressiveness of the eastern slum-Jew immigrant, dumped into America yearly in such great numbers. That is more even than human beings—who are, when not artificially agitated, the most stoical and patient of all the animal creation—can comfortably bear. So a twinge of anti-Semitism occurs in response—and of course the good Jew suffers along with the bad, just as in the past the intelligent Anglo-Saxon American has suffered because of the bad manners of herds of preposterous Babbitts sightseeing in Europe.

In order not to jump to conclusions regarding what must seem to the Anglo-Saxon a particularly harsh intolerance, the situation of the Jewish community in *Mitteleuropa*—that is in Germany, Austria, Poland, Czechoslovakia, Hungary, Romania and the Baltic States—must be fully taken into account. Popular prejudice is very powerful still in all those countries—as an *Agitationsmittel*, or instrument of political agitation, anti-Semitism is highly effective. It is not only the Hitlerites—every shade of Nationalist is in one degree or another anti-Semitic. The enemies of Hitlerism accuse the leaders of that party of making a cynical use of this handy weapon of race-antagonism for their own ends. I do not believe that that is the case, so far at all events as Hitler himself is concerned.

One of the principal opponents of Hitlerism, the Austrian, Graf R.N. Coudenhove-Kalergi (who is a prominent anti-antisemite also), writing of the assassination of Rathenau, makes the following assertion: "Rathenau...wurde in erster Linie nicht darum ermordet, weil er Verständigungspolitik trieb—sondern weil er Jude war."[5]

This is no doubt true. Whether socialist or monarchist, the German inherits this very powerful prejudice: he identifies the Jew with everything that is inimical to the society to which he belongs—the political and cultural system of the Aryan World. To deal with this situation Anti-antisemitic Societies have recently been formed. The principal one has its offices in Paris. (Mr. H.G. Wells is a member of its committee.) The young Berlin leader of the National Socialists, Goebbels (*Angriff*, December 5th, 1930), in a reply to the editor of the *Matin* (who had, in an anti-antisemitic

---

[5] "Rathenau...was not murdered primarily because he pursued a policy of understanding—but because he was a Jew."

magazine described the Jews as "a spiritual and cultural elite"), wrote as follows:

> Vielleicht überzeugt er sich einmal in Berlin, dem Hauptbetätigungsfeld dieser "Elite," wie sich ihre Kultur in Jazz, Negertänzen und ähnlichen Ergüssen, die uns vollkommen wesensfremd sind äussert.[6]

So it goes on, a battle of ideas, with people of Jewish origin always identified with the tendencies that are destructive of the European, or "Aryan," ethos. And it is perhaps only fair to the National Socialist to say that the Jew has often lent color to these accusations. But the Jew no doubt would retort that, corning as he generally does from Tartary, he cannot be expected to be much attracted by carol-singing, protestant hymn-music, or the Teutonic Royal-Academicism of official painting, and that in any case he buys and sells—being a man of affairs—novelties that are good business propositions. He might go more deeply into it than that, of course, and protest that it was not he at all, but the great "Aryan" inventors and technicians, who have been responsible for all the destructive modernism of the present Western World. Western Science is to blame, in short. He has made use of this (he could point out with some show of reason) but would of his own accord never have *invented* it.

I will not pursue this argument: but we will suppose that as we turn away we have heard the National Socialist demanding angrily what suspension bridges, telephones, and elevators, in themselves, have necessarily to do with Jazz and Negro Art; and (to give the Jew the last word) we can imagine that we hear him in his turn pointing out, always to some effect, that as to the latter, is it not the Negro, in the Land of Elevators, who is employed to operate

---

[6] "Perhaps he'd like to convince himself one of these days in Berlin, the principal field of activity of this "Elite," how their culture, in Jazz, Nigger-dances, and similar amusements (which are completely alien to us), expresses itself."

same? So the music of ex-slaves gets mixed up, not unnaturally after all, with the modernist machinery, employed to whisk cartloads of Babbitts up and down their megalopolitan steel and concrete towers. But we should immediately hear the National Socialist insisting that this New York civilization was rather Judeo-American than European-American. All the replies, and counter-replies, however, of this fierce dispute, we will allow to die away.

As to England. Someone has to govern England, it must be conceded, now that the Normans have faded out, and that the Irish have thrown up the job and decided to settle down in a well-earned obscurity, upon their own private bogs, locking themselves up politically with their local Island politics—washing their hands finally of this ungrateful Anglo-Saxon land. I might even agree (without prejudice) that indeed the Jews (first of all having obtained the tacit consent—not at all dearly bought, I think—of Mr. Bernard Shaw and myself) govern England to the complete satisfaction of everybody, and without a hitch, or so much as a single rift in the lute! But that would not be quite true: for if indeed, wearing the trousers, the Jew is the brilliant and bossy *Hausfrau* of this stolid English hubby, the latter has at least, in his quiet way, succeeded in influencing her, decidedly for the good. In short, upon that hypothesis, is not the Jew here, from the Hitler standpoint, disinfected and anglicized? Just as in the States he has been transformed (that yankee Abraham or "Abie") into a true Western product—presented, to crown everything, with a wild white Irish Rose! How, under such circumstances, could Abie "remember Carthage?" It would be against nature to dream (too much) of Zion—with Kathleen Na Hoolan crooning away in his ear!

What an Englishman or an American friendly to Hitler should perhaps say is this. He should say to the Hitlerite that he takes the Jew too seriously: *"For better or for worse,"* in the words of the English marriage service, there *is* the Jew! Feminine, and in many ways very unpleasant—all people have their bad sides—yet some *modus vivendi* has to be found; and as a middleman of uncanny penetration, may he not even have an important civilizing function? Then of course this traditional Jewish figure, of melodrama or of comedy, tends to disappear the farther West it travels. In *Mitteleuropa* everyone has seen, as a daily sight and familiar object, this Jew of stage-tradition. But I do not really suppose that in England any one has even clapped eyes upon a proper Jew since the days of Dickens. The Jew is almost become for us a Shakespearian myth out of *The Merchant of Venice*. Therefore it is unprofitable to talk to the Englishman about "The Jewish Question." It is no use (as did the *Völkische Beobachter* at the time of the appointment) to reproach the English because Sir Isaac Isaacs is made governor-general of Australia. You cannot de-cosmopolitanize the British Empire—whether that would be desirable or not is another question, of course.

From all this emerges principally two things, I think. The Hitlerite must understand that, when he is talking to an Englishman or an American about "The Jew" (as he is prone to do), he is apt to be talking about that gentleman's wife! Or anyhow *"Chacun son Jew!"* is a good old English saying. So if the Hitlerite desires to win the ear of England he must lower his voice and coo (rather than shout) *Juda verrecke!*—if he must give expression to such a fiery intolerant notion. Therefore—a pinch of malice certainly, but no anti-Semitism for the love of Mike!

But on the other hand, to the Anglo-Saxon I would say: Do not allow these difficult matters to sway you too much (though decidedly warning this crude Teuton to be civil, when in your company). But still allow a little *Blutsgefühl* to have its way (a blood-feeling towards this other mind and body like your own)— in favor of this brave and very unhappy impoverished kinsman. Do not allow a mere bagatelle of a *Judenfrage* to stand in the way of that!

Now I think I have said all that need be said, in reconciliation of the various susceptibilities involved, and shall be able to proceed without interference from this particular racial red-herring.

Adolf Hitler a Man of Peace

———◆———

Hitler is The German Man, therefore Hitler is a Man of Peace—so I asserted just now, and so I have done again in the heading of this chapter. But I must go into this in greater detail if I am to substantiate such a paradox. It is, I suppose, not much use just saying that the "Boche" is in his heart "a Man of Peace," and leaving it at that. For the "war-guilt-lie," as the Germans call it, not only involves the late rulers of Germany. The whole German People were regarded, so very recently, thanks to the Allied propaganda department, as a swarm of ferocious Huns, that it would be too much to hope that the average Anglo-Saxon reader would accept the theory of Adolf Hitler being a sucking-dove, merely *because* he was a "Boche!"

Now that we have got down to the root of Hitlerism—namely Herr Hitler himself—let us take Hitler in his role of nationalist, and then consider what that nationalism may portend for the rest of Europe. That is, after all, what we mainly want to find out.

First, as I stated in an earlier chapter, the militancy of the Hitlerist will be misunderstood if it is identified in any way with that of the Action Française. Self-conscious Gallic nationalism today is a very frail thing indeed. A handful of Catholic royalists—that is the Action Française movement. It is true that recently it has shown a tendency to grow, perhaps in sympathy with Hitlerism. But it is still a Parisian political fad, rather than a National Movement.

The nationalism of Adolf Hitler is, it must always be remembered, National *Socialism*. It is the militancy of an armed peasant, not the aristocratic militancy of a dispossessed aristocratic class; or that of a royalist intellectual, of aristocratic disposition, like Charles Maurras. Then regarded historically, and in the light of post-war practical politics, the nationalism of the

Action Française (that of Charles Maurras and of Leon Daudet) in its dogmatic anti-Germanism, has always seemed to me, I confess, unrealistic: and (in the light of our immediate political necessities) all wrong. Similarly, the Gallicism of Monsieur Coty, the founder of *L' Ami du Peuple*, suffered from an automatic phobia against the traditional enemy across the Rhine. These nationalist phobias, if carried to their logical conclusion, could only end in the complete "Balkanization" of Europe. And that Balkanization is already far too far advanced for an intelligent observer to feel sympathy with any man who seemed likely to accelerate it.

It is because I believe that Hitler is *not* a "nationalist" of that Balkanizing order that I am interested in the Hitler movement. I believe that he, and his associates, may have a true prescription embedded in the heart of their doctrine, for a nationalism that would be wider and more intelligent than that of the Action Française or than that of Mussolini.

This belief I base upon certain statements of Hitler. They have sounded far more intelligent than one is accustomed to expect from nationalist dictators. Hitler has even of late experienced some difficulty with the more conventional of his followers, especially in the matter of France. These malcontents objected that the friendly remarks of their leader upon the subject of France, and his dispatch of olive branches to Paris, smacked of the unpatriotic, even of an un-German attitude to the secular enemy of the German people. Those were evidently short-sighted Junker objections.

It is essential to understand that Adolf Hitler is not a saber-rattler at all. Indeed, he uses all his influence to prevent his followers from engaging in stupid nationalist demonstrations against France or against Poland. Thus, some weeks since, when it was announced that the police had rounded up a group of armed National Socialists about three hundred strong, camped upon an estate near the Polish frontier, Hitler immediately repudiated them. If they were National Socialists, he said, or if any member of the N.S.D.A.P. should be found among them, they would immediately be expelled from the party. Any National Socialist carrying firearms is expelled from the party—that is the order that has gone out since the September elections: and in any adventures of the sort described, National Socialists have been absolutely forbidden to engage. But it turned out in the end that among three hundred persons arrested, only three were (or once had been) National Socialists.

But it must appear strange to the English reader (accustomed to the rather lurid accounts in the English Press of Herr Hitler's activities) to find him represented here as a Man of Peace, or at all events not as a simple straightforward nationalist fire-eater. Nevertheless such, I am persuaded, is the case. Hitler is *not* a straightforward, simple, fire-eating, true-blue, saber-rattling, mustachioed puppet at all. I do not think that if Hitler had his way, he would bring the fire and the sword across otherwise peaceful frontiers. He would, I am positive, remain peacefully at home, fully occupied with the internal problems of the *Dritte Reich*. And as regards, again, the vexed question of the anti-Semitic policy of his party, in that also I believe Hitler himself—once he had obtained power—would show increasing moderation and tolerance. In the *Dritte Reich*, as conceived by Hitler, that great Jewish man of science, Einstein, would, I think, be honored as he deserves. On the other hand, those destructive financial buffoons, the Schlarek Brothers (who played such colossal Capone-like pranks, turning upside-down the municipal world of Berlin—preparing the way indeed for the first great National Socialist successes in that city—divine rogues as they no doubt are and all that, but politically a first-class nuisance) *they* would, I imagine, be asked *to go to Chicago*—in the sense of *Go to Bath!* or something of that sort. (Would not *Go to Chicago!* serve as a useful modern equivalent for that expletive? There are so many people everywhere who ought to *Go to Chicago* if not exactly to *take a ride!*)

Hitler is a prophet, like Muhammad, Mussolini, or Lenin. Personally, everyone is at liberty to prefer the Arab, or the Italian, or the Russian. But here at least is the German variety.

The personal character of the prophet is a thing of first-rate importance, in estimating what this particular great stirring of a people that is called a "movement" (that is to say, an instinctive rather than a reasoned thing) may ultimately signify for the rest of the world. But Hitler is so *typical*: so the German character in general comes into it as well. One feels, should he fall tomorrow, the movement could still proceed without him. He is a truly socialist prophet—an armed socialist prophet, his originality lies in that.

Hitler addressed a great meeting of the academic youth of Berlin at the *"Neue Welt"* last December. The following passage in a newspaper account of this event will serve to bring out the true nature of the Hitler message, as conceived by a Hitler partisan:

> Dann spricht Adolf Hitler. Mit der ganzen Wucht seiner gewaltigen Persönlichkeit, aber gebändigt durch die Zügel einer aus dem Leben geborenen und darum wahrhaft lebendigen Philosophie. Oft ist es nicht leicht, den vorgetragenen Gedanken bis in ihre letzten Tiefen hinein zu folgen. Wann bekommt der Student je vom Katheder aus eine so umfassende Fülle universaler Gedanken vermittelt? Dazu müssen sie schon, statt zu ihren hochgelehrten Professoren, zu dem einfachen Mann aus dem Volke kommen, der nicht als Weisheitsautomat totes Wissen predigt, sondern natürliches Leben...[7]

---

[7] "Thus Adolf Hitler speaks. With all the fire of his powerful personality, but held in check by a philosophy, issuing from the very soil of life, and hence truly living. Often it is not easy to follow the thoughts presented to their ultimate depths. When has the student ever had communicated to him, from the professorial pulpit, such an all-embracing fullness of universal Thought? For that, in place of their high-learned professors, they must come to the simple Man

Hitler is here presented as "the simple Man of the People," who is no "philosophic automaton" (such as the "high-learned professors" to which the assembled academic youth is accustomed) teaching "dead wisdom," but on the contrary possessed of the natural wisdom of life.

So it is not only as the German Man, but as the Natural Man, that Hitler is to be regarded, according to his enthusiastic followers.

"Hitler ist unstreitig eine grosse und echte Persönlichkeit... zweifellos eine der grössten, die wir überhaupt im politischen Leben Deutschlands besitzen."[8] This is the judgment of the writer I have quoted elsewhere (Junius Alter), who is not himself a fanatical nationalist by any means. A "great and genuine personality" this German *Bauarbeiter*[9] seems from all accounts to be: and so it would be a great mistake to regard him as merely just another dictator: for he is a very different person from Mussolini, Pilsudski, or Primo de Rivera, and we must expect very different behavior to ensue upon his accession to power, if that ever happens, than what has occurred as a result of the other European dictatorships.

---

of the People-who does not teach dead knowledge, like a philosophic automaton, but the real stuff of life..."
[8] "Hitler is indisputably a great and genuine personality...undoubtedly one of the greatest we have in the political life of Germany at all."
[9] Construction worker

Hitler an "Armed Prophet"

"All armed prophets have conquered, and the unarmed ones have been destroyed."

Machiavelli, *The Prince*

Having declared my opinion, that Hitler is not a gratuitously warlike individual at all, it is incumbent upon me next to show that the military nature of the organization of his party does not conflict with that description. For an armed man-of-peace is likely to prove a nonsense.

No great parliamentary party in modern England has ever so far possessed a private militia. It is not easy for an Englishman to imagine such a thing an American, accustomed to Tammany politics, could conceive this more easily). A party with a gymnasium-drilled, militant, partisan force, raised for riot-breaking or for offensives in street-war, at its back, may yet enter the Mother of Parliaments. But I hope not.

Meanwhile, for a revolutionary party today in Germany, that is absolutely necessary. Such a movement as Hitler's enlists muscle, perforce, and its levies are trained in attack and defense: if it attempted to stage its disagreeable views unbacked by a ring of fists, relying solely upon police protection for the safety of its platform, or of its party premises, it would be laid out flat within a week. The entire personnel, from the prophet downwards to the last party-typist, would be put out of action, and that by terror backed by firearms—and as I have said the German communist is given *carte blanche* when such a rival revolutionary organization is in question—or at least that is what the Nazis say. The Prussian police think like the American police: let vermin wipe out vermin. Also, it is said that many *Schupos* are communist—policemen must be something.

Nazis are less the *Gesinnungsgenossen*[10] of the police than are the Red party-boys of the redfrontfighting squads. Again, the police cannot be everywhere—even if a Republican police president so desired it.

Hitler has, in consequence of all this, been compelled from the start (these measures date from years back—from mug-battles in beer—cellars in Munich) to constitute his own *Schutzpolizei*—for his *Sturmabteilungen* or civil "storm-detachments" are much more a picked police-force than an amateur or unconstitutional military organization.

Regimes such as the Spanish, Italian or the Russian, repose ultimately upon the armed threat of a picked force of police. The Civil Guard holds down Spain—the Ogpu Police holds down Russia—in both instances with rifles and machine-guns. The Franco revolt[11] in Spain was broken by the Civil Guard. The German *Schupo* holds down the Reds and the Nazis. But in Russia or Italy no such thing as a bodyguard of an opposition-leader would be possible since no opposition is tolerated.

But in democratic countries, ornamented with parliaments, that has to be allowed. You would give the show away if you did not. So before the overthrow of the parliaments-on-the-British-Model, the most powerful rebels have their militias—such as the Camelots du Roi in Paris, the Nazis in Germany, or the Marxists in all democratic countries. That is understood. You cannot stop it. "Fair play's a jewel" (an English proverb).

To the extent detailed above Hitler is an armed prophet. But he has behind him today a hundred thousand fists—mere knuckles not knuckle-dusters. There is no armed private militia. No machine-guns or hidden store of arms exist, that is almost certain.

---

[10] Like-minded people

[11] In December 1930, Ramón Franco, brother of the more famous Francisco Franco, flew over Madrid and dropped leaflets which announced that a republican revolution had broken out, calling on citizens and soldiers to aid the rising.

For if there had been, long ago they would have been detected and confiscated by the police.

In Austria, the Prince of Starhemberg has, according to all accounts, a considerable arsenal upon his private estates, and maintains the nucleus of a *Heimwehr* army-corps this daring Prince is the leader of the militant Austrian nationalists, allies of Hitler's). But Hitler, it is I think quite certain, has nothing of the sort, nor could he if he wished. The Prussian Republican Administration is a much uglier customer to deal with than the easy-going Viennese.

Nur legal!—only by *legal* means—is the watchword of the Nazis today. There is no question of an armed rising or of a *Putsch*, or coup d'état. When the majority of the electors are in favor of a policy (or when such a majority may be confidently expected in the near future) why attempt to carry that policy through by violent and uncertain means? That would indeed be a senseless proceeding! The present Hitlerist attitude is adamantly pacific. The orders that have gone out to confine themselves to *legal* measures only, of propaganda and of self-defense, are very strictly enforced, within the party-ranks.

There is another matter upon which it is necessary, so it seems, to give some enlightenment: namely, the question, so often asked, whether Germany contemplates a War of Revenge. Are not the Hitlerist "storm detachments" from that point of view an international danger? This is as a matter of fact a complete absurdity. The military power of France today is so overwhelming, and Germany has been so scrupulously disarmed, that such an eventuality as a War of Revenge—or even, if the French were not there, an attack upon Poland about the famous corridor—would be like asking a naked unarmed man to make a frontal attack upon a machine-gun nest (with a cloud of bomb-bearing airplanes circling overhead). The idea, in short, of Germany being a military menace can be entirely dismissed from the most apprehensive mind—although it is true that the Paris Press is forever scribbling away about it, their purpose in doing so depending, no doubt, upon the political situation in France at the moment. But they always consider it useful to insist that Germany is a great menace—that is good for the armament firms.

These anxieties having been allayed, there remains the fact that the Hitler Party is organized upon military lines. That is so, of course. And no doubt—if arms were available, as they are not—its well-disciplined partisans would constitute a dangerous force. To this extent Hitler is potentially an "armed prophet." But the Hitlerist is much too pre-occupied with those whom he regards as enemies within the German frontiers, to have much time to think about those without.

To be Masters of the Street before being Masters of the State—that is recognized as a necessity by the present-day German politician. The Democrats have been taken unawares. They have not been able to deal with the Nazi because of his Mastery of the Street. At present, street-fighting forces are being feverishly organized (with a communist stiffening) to fight him there.

The Marxists train their people in the art of civil war: and the gentle art of *street-fighting* is one of the main features of their instruction, as is well known. So, whoever it may be, who would be free to speak, in street or in conference-hall, to his fellow-citizens, has eventually got to fight in the street—or in the hall.

But these battles must be, upon their side—so say the Nazis—*Nur legal*. "*Natürlich, nur legal!*" And accepting this severe handicap, their scuffling is generally conducted in as "legal" a manner as possible.

Here is a brief statement upon the policy of *legal* violence as a measure of defense. It is the handiwork of a "storm-leader," taken from a little pamphlet upon the aims of National Socialism:

> Together with the general membership organization, there arose for the protection of large mass-meetings, against the attacks of Marxists, a special party police-service, which fundamentally

comprised only young men, with the object of breaking terror by means of terror. Hitler wrote: "The young movement stood from the beginning for the principle that its doctrine should be advanced by spiritual means, but that the protection of this teaching must also be secured, when necessary, by physical means."

The abovementioned defense-service, after a free fight at a meeting in the Munich *Hofbräuhaus*, when Marxists tried to break up a meeting of National Socialists—at that time the movement had not long been born—received the name of *Storm-detachments S.A.*, in memory of the "heroic onset of the at that time mere handful." With its growth, this function of the movement was developed. Obviously, it can be no armed movement, for Hitler understood, that with present-day requirements, no soldier can be created by means of a weekly, or two-hourly, training. The S.A. must also be no secret organization, since the National Socialist Movement needs not a hunched or two hundred reckless confederate partisans, but a hundred thousand and yet again a hundred thousand fanatical fighters for the National Socialist worldview.

Not in secret conventicles shall it be affected, but in powerful mass demonstrations—not through dagger, poison, or pistol, can the path of the movement be opened up, but though the Mastery of the Street. We have to convince the Marxist that the future Lord of the Street is National Socialism, just as one day it will the Lord of the State.

The S.A. still works today according to these precepts of Hitler. They are, whether in election-struggles or for the other propagandist activities of the closely-disciplined party, the rigid backbone of our movement.

Hitler's words in the above passage are worth noting—*Not in secret conventicles*—in the Camorra of a militant minority, in fact—but in open, hundred-thousand-strong, visible masses of the citizenry, are National Socialist ends to be achieved. Not by means of dagger, poison, or pistol, also, must the Hitlerist seek to impose his political views upon the people. Terror is abjured—secrecy is discouraged. Force, however, to some extent must be employed. And the Hitler-police have carried out their duties with great energy.

"All armed prophets have conquered," Machiavelli asserts. An *unarmed* prophet today would certainly be just about as impossible a proposition as in the days of the *Condottiere*. There is still some instruction in Machiavelli: I will quote a passage now from the sixth chapter of his *Prince* (*Everyman* edition):

> The difficulties that (Princes) have in acquiring (their principality) arise in part from the new rules and methods which they are forced to introduce to establish their government and its security. And it ought to be remembered that there is nothing more difficult to take in hand, more perilous to conduct, or more uncertain in its success, than to take the lead in the introduction of a new order of things. Because the innovator has for enemies all those who have done well under the old conditions, and lukewarm defenders in those who may do well under the new. This coolness arises partly from fear of the opponents, who have the laws on their side, and partly from the incredulity of men, who do not readily believe in new things until they have had a long experience of them. Thus, it happens that whenever those who are hostile have the opportunity to attack, they do it like partisans, whilst the others defend lukewarmly, in such wise that the prince is endangered along with them.
>
> It is necessary, therefore, if we desire to discuss this matter thoroughly, to inquire whether these innovators can rely on themselves or have to depend on others: that is to say, whether, to consummate their enterprise, have they to use prayers or can they use force? In the first instance they always succeed badly, and never compass anything: but when they can rely on themselves and use force, then they are rarely endangered. Hence it is that all armed prophets have conquered, and the unarmed ones been destroyed. Besides the reasons mentioned, the nature of the people is variable, and whilst it is easy to persuade them, it is difficult to fix them in that persuasion. And thus, it is necessary to take such

measures that, when they believe no longer, it may be possible to make them believe by force.

The immediate objective of the Hitler Party is to turn out the present Socialist Government of Prussia. They have their eyes riveted upon Prussia. By means of new elections, they will secure an effective majority in the Prussian Parliament; that is the first step. "Whoever holds Prussia holds the Reich!" they say. They then would have the Prussian Police in their hands. It would be filled with Nazis (the unofficial police would become official police). If they doubled their vote in a further Reichstag Election, they could no longer be cheated of power, all the armed forces of the country would be in their hands—*Reichswehr* plus Police. They then would, by these *strictly legal*, beautifully parliamentary, wholly democratic, means, establish a National Socialist dictatorship. Thus—the legal authority conferred upon him by the German People—Hitler would become in the full sense "an armed prophet." That is the plan. And that it is essential for him to be if his movement is to succeed.

In a book published by the Labour Publishing Co. in 1923, *Fascism* (by Odon Por, translated by E. Townshend), the following passage from *The National Being* by A.E. is quoted:

> Our modern States have not yet succeeded in building up that true national life where all feel the identity of interest; where the true social or civic feeling is engendered and the individual bends all his efforts to the success of the community on which his own depends; where, in fact, the ancient Greek conception of citizenship is realized, and individuals are created who are conscious of the identity of interest between themselves and their race.

The *creation of individuals*, who, according to the Greek conception of citizenship, are "conscious of *the identity of interest between themselves and their race*"—that is the task that the

Hitler Movement has set itself. That no such consciousness exists in Anglo-Saxon countries I need hardly tell you. But in Germany for many years some such consciousness has been in existence, so it does not have to be created so much as organized anew, in response to the needs of the moment. It is thanks to this organized consciousness among the Germans that unconstitutional compulsion does not have to be exercised. *Force*—in the Communist, or the Machiavelli, sense—is not necessary.

I think now that I have covered most of the ground necessary to give you a good idea of the status of National Socialism in the present parliamentary regime in Germany. Most of their militancy is forced upon them, I believe. Their attitude to force is, I think, by no means *energumène*. Their hefty young street-fighting warriors have not the blood-shot eyes and furtive manners of the political gutter-gunman, but the personal neatness, the clear blue eyes, of the police! The Anglo-Saxon would feel reassured at once in the presence of these straightforward young pillars of the law. Everything is strictly legal—*nur legal!*—fair, square and above-board to the letter.

PART III
RACE AND CLASS

Many "Class Wars"

In their *Programm* the National Socialists catalogue our Chaos—it is "a picture of a battle of all against all." The Revelation of St. John the Divine does not provide a more chaotic scene, of dream-like universal conflict, than what we now witness all about us, everywhere in the world. This carefully planned system of conflicts—of "class wars"—is plotted like the checkerboard patches of a garden, designed to represent a wilderness of misspent human ingenuity.

These "wars" are forever simmering. As we have seen in the case of the political life of Germany, a savage ferment prevails, above the muffled roar of which pistol shots ring out, and daily the dead and wounded are carried away to morgue or hospital. It does not require phenomenal foresight to discern that at any moment this universal unrest could be made to swell up suddenly into a world-storm of unparalleled proportions—a "War-to-end-Class War" as it were. And the more classes that are contrived, the more likelihood of some ultimate Civil Armageddon to abolish them.

The class war was an excellent notion. Its applications are far wider than are generally supposed, for there is scarcely anything in the world that you cannot make into a *class*. And wherever you have a *class*, there you can have a *war*. As the N.S.D.A.P. *Programm* describes it:

> The picture of a fight of *all against all*. Government against people, party against party, thereby resulting in the strangest and most impossible alliances, parliament against government, employee against employer, consumer against producer, trader against producer and consumer, landlord against householder,

workman against peasant, official against public, working-class against "Bourgeoisie," Church against State...

And all this fine work, they exclaim, is the handiwork of our little friend Marx, and is kept alive and further developed, at the cost of uncounted outpourings of money—for the agitator's salary to finance political strikes, and so forth. This is the business of the "Marxist," as the German calls him.

We will not argue here the pros and cons of Marxism. All revolutions are means to ends. Experience tells us that the ends are usually not found to justify the means. It is a matter of opinion. But what we can do—neglecting the theoretic ends at which the Marxist aims—is to amplify a little the civic picture of catastrophic disintegration.

Everyone is at all events aware of the existence of these interlocking chains and concatenations of domestic "wars" between (often quite imaginary, or artificial) classes. Many of these, minor or major, class wars have their newspaper-name. Thus, everybody is quite familiar with the term "sex war." And a very bad "war" that can be, when some poor uneducated couple are stirred up by newspaper slogans and "provocative" sex-warlike propaganda, and fall upon each other: a war of attrition begins a trench warfare with beds and bolsters and coal-scuttles as the familiar objects of the battle-field. All the normal strife of loving couples is embittered a thousand-fold.

Let us take this particular "class war" and scrutinize it a little more closely than is generally done in, say, the Sunday illustrated paper. Marx must step back—he cannot be held responsible for its start, at least. We find at once that the sex war is coeval with that great web of revolutionary humanitarian movements—in the early skirmishes of which Dickens, for instance, in England, played such a spirited part, and on behalf of which (over half a century later) we see Strindberg so hard at work up in Sweden—but in his case upon the other side. This particular "War" started before

Marx's time. It was before he produced his evil formula, "class war."

As a movement of humanitarian liberation these "wars" of brother against brother at first were not necessarily evil, though conducted at times with a farcical silliness. Also, they were *domestic* disputes and feuds. They were the monopoly—even the secret—of the European World. The immemorial institutions of the East were not, for a long while, disturbed by our feverish unrest—but now the whole Earth looks on, with delight, hatred, and scorn (or actively participates) in the inner readjustments of our social system. It would have been better to keep these adjustments strictly private and domestic.

This broadcast and cosmic advertisement, so much gratuitous publicity, for domestic issues, is reminiscent of another stupidity—namely, the use of great numbers of Asiatic and African troops in the War—*stupid*, that is, if you desire the good of Europe—*intelligent* if you desire its destruction.

I am not so much arguing here that the European civilization ought not to end, as merely pointing out *how* that destruction is being brought about. It is a subject of constant speculation how the Roman Empire came to collapse—some say Christianity, others say mosquitoes. There is no mystery at all—it is an open conspiracy—about the Fall of Europe. In a word, it is the result, in the first instance, of an enormous new factor—machinery and industrial technique. In the short space of a century science turned our world upside-down. Secondly, the world being upside-down and inside-out, the shrewd parasite (existing in all times and places) psychologically an outcast as regards our settled structure, took advantage of this disorder and consequent bafflement to sting us all to death. Of course, historians in the future will assert that it was influenza, or the pranks of the last Roman Kaiser. But we know better.

To return to the good old class wars by which we are beset, many beyond question originated in bad abuses, or else were the logical outcome of a regrouping necessitated, by the conditions of the Industrial Age. For instance, a *really* intellectual woman was surely right to free herself from a stupid and overbearing husband. Surely there was nothing against her possessing a separate estate? If instead of bearing children she preferred to run a shop or factory, why not? And so forth. Child-labor in the mills was a monstrosity because it produced monsters, and because the mill-owners who took it for granted were monsters. Has there ever been a human society free of great abuses deserving upheavals? And the Industrial Age did shake our society like an earthquake; it loosened its structure, and, as it imposed upon everybody new conditions of life, it set up a natural conflict between those with imagination and spare energy, who wanted to go quick, and those who resented the new, and wanted to go slow, or not at all. So, it is not any too easy to discuss, without misunderstanding, the policy of these Civil Wars or class wars, which honeycomb our Western democratic communities today.

This ferment did well till it got into the hands of the crook: he always seizes upon a weak inflamed spot in a society to do some mischief and extract some loot. The *Geldmensch*[12] and his satellite the Agitator were soon on the job. They organized these masses of people in disequilibrium—displaced and uprooted as a consequence of the Industrial Revolution. They organized them into classes. There was nothing they did not fake up into a class. And they manufactured and stuck upon each class they had isolated and organized, a label, or a ticket: they might have been cattle.

These labels were usually *good* or *bad* labels; they took with them stern reproof or saponaceous flattery. (The *Geldmensch* and the Agitator are always strongly *moralistic* in their outlook. They are *very* fervent. They find that it invariably pays to have a sickly moral huskiness in the throat—the rankest sobstuff is worth its

---

[12] "Money Man" i.e. "Merchant"

weight in banknotes, given the psychological moment). Well, there it was: they found they could traffic endlessly in these animosities. *Divide et impera* is the best trade-device, as well as political, and a roaring trade was done, beyond question.

When *two nations* fall out, the armament-king and chemical-king rake in the shekels. When two men fall out, the lawyer coins money. When two *classes* fall out, it is the same thing. Power, or wealth, passes from both to some *third* class.

The Versailles Treaty Makers must have known that the more nations you make (or break the world up into) the more jolly old profitable disputes you prepare—the more pickings for the Outsider. Who gains? Always some Mr. X. the Third Party, the Outsider. England, as an island power, was *The Outsider*, or the Third Party, for some time—she sold munitions to foreign nations at war. But today it is no nation of course, since capital is international.

Then the manufacture of endless class wars was both profitable, destructive, and awfully amusing. It had amusement-value—it had news-value—it was good business. And it has been the only visible means of support of millions of men for many, many years now, and they have waxed fat upon it—some come to see me to ask me to have a slap at some "Class" or other they are fixing up, and they can scarcely get in at my modest door.

But the class-combatants—though they may start full of honorable motives, and be excited to action by some fantastic injustice—end up, under these conditions, in a more and more squalid, long-drawn-out, poison gas campaign. And at the end, there they are—*both* will inevitably be bankrupt of energy—both are defeated—knocked-out by the *Third Party*. The Hon. Mr. X. (or Lord) and his Provocative Agents.

But people are taught nothing about all this at school. They would be very difficult to manage if they knew all this, and I agree that they ought to know nothing. And of course there is this to be said, if you told it them (in a take-it-or-leave-it, non-religious, democratic manner) they would not understand it, and if they understood they would not believe. I am not saying the *Geldmensch* should not profit by this human helplessness. I am just pointing out to you—if you have eyes to see—how it all happens: and I am explaining for what it is worth that there is a large and powerful party in Germany who see it too, more or less, and who identify themselves, for some reason, with the helpless herds, and who have a most terrible down on the *Geldmensch*, as they call him.

THE ART OF BEING RULED

When in 1926 *The Art of Being Ruled* (Chatto & Windus) was published, no one was prepared for such a radical statement of the new post-war situation in the world, it seems, and there was not such competition as one might have anticipated, among the more dashing critics, to rush in and discuss it, and so today it still costs 18s.—and the poor cannot read it at all. Therefore it is my habit to lift from it (I am not the only person who does the lifting either, from that inaccessible volume) for my more accessible and popular books, relevant passages; especially when I should, by not doing so, merely be covering old ground. So, at this point I will introduce some expository extracts from that book, for it is certain that they will throw a great deal of light upon what we are at present discussing. Here then is a quotation (Part IV. Chapter III. *Art of Being Ruled*): it will explain the relation of race to class:

> It may be well to go for a moment into the relation between class and race in the formation of the former. The classes that have been parasitic on other classes have always in the past been *races*. The class-privilege has been a race-privilege. Every white man until recently has been in full possession of a race-privilege where other races of other colors were concerned, which constituted the white man as a class. The privilege was never developed to the extent that the Achaean race-privilege of the Athenian citizen, for example, was. But in a general way it formed part of the consciousness of the white man. Cleanliness was next to godliness, and whiteness was the indispensable condition of cleanliness. So to be a chosen people was to be a white people.
>
> This class element in race expressed itself in the application of the term lady, for instance, to the most modest citizens of the Anglo-Saxon race. The *Lady* in *charlady* is a race courtesy-title. It is a class-title that it was possible for her to exact on the score

of *race*. This rudimentary fact very few poor whites have understood. They have been inclined to take these small but precious advantages for granted, as indicative of a *real* superiority, not one resulting, as in fact it did, from the success of the organized society to which they belonged. They have confused class with race—somewhat to their undoing.

Today race and color are as distinctive features as ever: and it is unlikely in the future that race will cease to play its part in the formation of class—as, again, many simple white people will discover to their great chagrin.

Or again, in the following page, discussing the *"race-origin of caste-feeling,"* I say:

The notion of the "gentleman" as we call it today is a race notion, originating in such things as Roman citizenship and its universal aristocratic privileges. The most absurd as well as degrading spectacle that this notion has ever provided was when the Roman citizen, in fact, was in question in the time of the Empire. All the wealth and the power of the Roman state passed more and more into the hands of alien freedmen. The Roman began rapidly to die out (the custom of child exposure contributed largely to this) and grew daily more impoverished. But the client-system kept those that remained just alive. The procedure of the allotment of food for the *sportula* of the client, and all the rest of the humiliating life of charity of the latest Romans, was carefully organized. So it came about that living as a numerous class of decayed gentility in the midst of the luxury and wealth of imperial Rome were most of the true Romans. One Emperor shipped a hundred thousand or so of them off to some colony. But there were still a good number of these proud, ragged remnants of republican Rome (or of cultivators of the surrounding land of original Italian stock driven to the city by the introduction of foreign slave-labor on the *latifundia*) remaining.

Class always takes with it the idea of race, then, and of some distant or recent conquest. How the notion of political personal freedom has spelled weakness in the end for Europe (so that it is not at all too much to say that that is the principal cause of its present decline) is that it is by way of this notion, through this gate, that all the disintegrating tendencies have entered.

There is a further passage that is apropos upon the same page (p. 115) which describes very clearly how class is an easy mechanical means of immobilizing—and so "governing," or it may be enslaving—the individual.

> Even if race were abolished by inter-mixture, it would still be possible, of course, to get your class-factor, and with it your organized war, by way of sex, age, occupational and other categories. "The intensity of organization is increased," as Mr. Russell points out, "when a man belongs to more organizations." The more classes (of which in their various functions he is representative) that you can make him become regularly conscious of, the more you can control him, the more of an automaton he becomes. Thus, if a man can be made to feel himself (a) an American, (b) a young American, (c) a middle-west young American, (d) a "radical and enlightened" middle-west young American, (e) a college-educated, etc. etc., (f) a college-educated dentist who is an etc. etc., (g) a college-educated dentist of such-and-such a school of dentistry, etc. etc.,—the more inflexible each of these links is, the more powerful, naturally, is the chain. Or he can be locked into any of these compartments as though by magic by anyone understanding the wires, in the way the Jesuit studied those things.

From these passages I think you will be able to see at once how the class-war notion, in all its innumerable applications, operates. There is almost no end to its uses. And if you consider for a moment the *power* any individual without illusions must possess, who is not himself amenable to these superstitions (especially if he has actually manufactured a few of them himself), then you will understand better how it happens that the world may come to be divided into those classified and ticketed out of existence, and those blamable ruffians who are the Mr. X—the great *Outsiders* in this hallucinated game.

You will not then have been initiated into the *Art of Being Ruled* in vain.

One Advantage in Race-Notion

What the National Socialist is, in reality, attempting to do, is to put *race* in the place of *class*. He says that the fact that a man is a sorter at the Post Office, or a metalworker, is not of such importance as that he is English, German, or French—or Chinese. Take a Chinese metalworker and a German metal-worker, for instance. The fact that both were metalworkers would not be so important as that the essential nature of one came out of all the past of China, and the essential nature of the other out of all the past of the White Northern races.

Does the notion of race supply as workable an ideology as that of class? It is impossible to answer that directly. If you make a fuss about the Celts, then it may be more attractive to the Irish metalworker to regard himself as a Celt than as a metal-worker. But at least it may be conceded that race is a more *inclusive* thing than class. Once a Celt, always a Celt—whatever Celt may be. But the metalworker may be a bookie's clerk tomorrow, and later on might take to the sea.

How much of what we call our personality comes to us from the countless people who have contributed to the production of us? Is it (1) possible, (2) desirable, that this past should be wiped out? I do not think we really have any choice in the matter. However, the class-doctrinaire has no greater enemy than race. And it is natural therefore that he should seek every opportunity of belittling race. It is also natural that the National Socialist, persuaded that the class-war propaganda is one of the main factors in the present disintegration—for it sets friend against friend—should insist upon race—and in Germany he has done that to some purpose (here it is only the stupidest of the stupid that would respond to anything of that sort).

The class-doctrine—as opposed to the race-doctrine—demands a *clean slate*. Everything must be wiped off slick. A sort of colorless, featureless, automaton—*temporally* two-dimensional—is what is required by the really fanatical Marxist autocrat. Nothing but a mind *without backgrounds*, without any spiritual depth, a flat mirror for propaganda, a parrot-soul to give back the catchwords, an ego *without reflection*, in a word, a sort of Peter Pan Machine—the adult child—will be tolerated.

The drawbacks, or rather the problems connected with the realization of the race-doctrine, I have dealt with in the section of this essay entitled "All that is not Race is Dross." The *extreme* interpretation of the race-doctrine would be liable to leave you with a romantic snob on your hands: the extreme interpretation of the class-doctrine with a simple robot.

What I think it is safe to affirm is that race, used as a propagandist engine, must tend to simplify and to concentrate. It promises political unity, at all events. It would, if followed out, draw people together, rather than thrust them apart—at least the people of the same race. Thus, it would secure greater social efficiency.

To demonstrate this, it is only necessary to point to the condition of the wife and husband under a regime ideologically based upon race, as opposed to the same couple under a regime based upon class (sex, of course, being one of the most important "classes" of all).

It must however be absolutely understood that there is no question of the Anglo-Saxon ever emulating this racialism' of the Germans. There is no occasion to go into the reasons for this. It is quite certain that it could not possibly happen. But class for that matter (except the traditional upper and lower class) is also not such a great success in England. That is no reason at all however why we should laugh at other people's ways of conducting their affairs, or not make the effort to fathom what they are driving at. There is nothing inherently ridiculous in race. It is simply a thing the Englishman takes no interest in, and that the American is bound to disregard—in the middle of the American "Melting-Pot."

PART IV

YOUTH–MOVEMENT BECOMES "HITLER–MOVEMENT"

The German Youth-Movement Becomes the "Hitler-Movement"

The human model for a thorough-going *Klassenmensch* or—"Class-person"—would be, so I remarked in the last chapter, a featureless, infantile robot—a mechanical infant-robot, without any mental or physical background at all. That is a standardized Peter Pan, who learns nothing and forgets everything—a phonograph for the convenient parrot-cries of the hour.

The rather childlike and slavish Russian nature may be purveying millions of such bearded infantile ecstatic Peter Pan parrots at this moment—I do not know. But that at all events is the *ideal*—it must be the ultimate result if it has not already happened.

In this connection the melting of the *Jugend Bewegung*, or Youth Movement, into the *Hitler Bewegung*, is of considerable interest. And of course, "youth-movement" has come to signify "age-war"—that is a Child-and-Parent War. In mild and pretty forms we are quite familiar with that war here too. The newspapers are as full of "age-war" articles, and Youth-at-the-Helm propaganda, as they have ever been of "sex war" articles. And the particular "class-war" based upon the "youth" mysticism has at once the most sinister and ridiculous results. Ten years ago, it popped a herd of old women into short knee-high show-girl skirts. It humbugs and afterwards distresses and unsettles a great number of politically over-simple adolescent persons—the fulsome flattery is taken *au pied de la letter*—and then as with other political flatteries, nothing happens, and youth grows restless and sad.

The meaning of the youth-propaganda is patent enough. In Big Business fewer and fewer individuals are *indispensable*. Less and less responsibility is shared by any given member of the more and more mechanical staff of underlings. A machine could usually do as well, or better, all the work that any average civil-servant or Big Business office-employee spends his life at (the postage-stamp machine does better and quicker what the employee behind the Post Office counter is doing half the time. The adding-machine does more efficiently the work of a bank clerk, etc. etc.).

Under these rapidly changing conditions, of mechanized business, the idea that seniority should spell higher wages is obsolete. Because a man is forty, he should, logically, have less—not more. This does not apply to many occupations, where experience, or personal initiative, still counts. But it *must* apply to all the great impersonal services—the offices of trusts, corporations, and government services. In them the man of forty should have less, not more, than at twenty—because he is an adding-machine, or a stamp-machine, or a sorting-machine, that is wearing out. The youth of twenty does exactly what he does, and he is fresher.

Under these circumstances the nonsense about experience, seniority, and all the things that were realities prior to the Machine Age, has to be knocked on the head. The newspapers are the property of the Big Business Barons—they are the *propaganda department*, as it were. Their debonair gossip—columns, even, with their disarming "chatterboxing," are put to the most serious political uses—all mixed up, of course, with what frocks Miss Chatterbox saw at the wedding of the Hon. Julia So-and-So.

What in fact the "age-war," or youth, articles are saying is just what I have said above. They are saying: "You old bald adding-machine of forty-odd, don't you come round and ask me for a rise next week! There's many a good strong youth of eighteen would be only too glad to do your work. I'll give the job to him for two pins. How I love youth! I'd like to see it at the helm—straight I would! As to you, you ought to be ashamed of yourself! Another word from you about *higher wages* and out you go—On the dole! See?"

YOUTH-MOVEMENT BECOMES "HITLER-MOVEMENT"

The fact that it is generally a pretty aged ruffian who is saying this or who is at the bottom of this maneuver, is neither here nor there. That makes it all the better fun.

We all know today why feminism came off (I am not now discussing the rights or wrongs of feminism—I am a feminist, of course: I am only discussing its great backing and its complete success). Women swarmed into the Big Business offices, shops, civil services. They did the very simple mechanical work such occupations entail just as well as the men they displaced. *And they got less pay.*

In England and America this same process is occurring with the youth-movement—age-war—lever. The newspapers, in other words the propaganda-department of the great Business Interests, have got busy everywhere, and there is little doubt that before long men's and women's wages will be on a diminishing scale, over, say, twenty-eight years old. At forty it will be the dole. For if man is to be used wholly as a machine, why is it possible to go on treating him as if he were something else? His "immortal soul" is all very well: but we, none of us believe much in that, do we, at this time of the day?

Here is a cutting from the *Daily Telegraph* (May 28th, 1929). *Homes for the Aged* at fifty is, I think, a euphemism, a breaking-it-gently: for having regard to what machines can do, and the daily output of new labor-saving appliances, and consequent huge unemployment, there is no reason to suppose that a man's effective working life can last longer than fifteen years—twenty years old to thirty-five, say—under the present capitalist system. However, here is the (rather out-of-date) *Daily Telegraph* statement:

HITLER

TOO OLD AT 50 IN U.S.A.

SUPER-EFFICIENCY VICTIMS

An Appeal for Pensions

"America is the richest country in the world," said Representative Hamilton Fish in the House of Representatives today: "but our wage-earners are left alone to worry and suffer the humiliation of poverty in their declining years." Mr. Fish urged that the time had arrived when the United States "shall cease playing the ostrich act and attempt to solve the serious problem of old-age dependency."

He proposes a special committee of five members, to be appointed by the Speaker of the House of Representatives, "to inquire into old-age pensions and study modern methods, by which practically all advanced nations of the world afford constructive relief to the worthy aged poor. American wage-earners of today," he said, "are thrown out on the industrial scrap-heap at middle-age, due to high pressure and to the super-efficiency methods of industrial plants, and the man or woman of fifty is unable to keep pace with younger workers."

He estimates that millions of American men and women, with families to support, are totally unable to save funds for old age, and declares the problem can only be solved by sound economical, constructive legislation.

Several State Legislatures, including New York, are now inquiring on similar lines. In a recent message to the Legislature, the Governor of the State of New York condemned the present method of dealing with the aged by means of alms-houses as antiquated, inefficient, expensive, and demoralizing.

In the above passage people are, I think, being let down a little too gently, for it is not at all likely that the employer of the future—whether that be an autocratic communist state, or present capitalism—is going to wait till a person is fifty to dismiss him. Nor is it likely that the Machine-soul of either communism or capitalism is going to support an obsolete and useless human machine in comfort and plenty up to a ripe old age.

The average man, I am sure, reading all that I have been saying above, would consider it a little joke of mine—a rather ferocious little joke—perhaps in bad taste somewhat—but still a harmless joke. But then he considers the articles he reads in the newspapers jokes as well. Is not the newspaper *his* newspaper (my morning paper)? The journalist is *his* buffoon. The reporter (or "our Special Correspondent" is the fellow who reports to him (for one penny a morning) what is going on in the world. And my word, doesn't he just see to it that those reports are correct to the letter?

Again, Mr. Everyman—or *L'homme moyen sensual*—the "average sensual man"—is a sentimentalist, and so he thinks everybody else is: about age—*his* age—he is very sentimental, and superstitious.

And in any attempt to convey to him the inner meaning of this particular "class-war" there lies the difficulty. To make him see that the sentimental angle is not the angle of everybody is none too easy. His "average sensuality" furnishes him with little glamors and softnesses that are far from being shared by the very hard-headed (and oh yes, hard-hearted) Big Business Elders who are occupied, *not* with the humdrum squalor of the average suburban life, but with somewhat more complicated considerations, and more extended horizons-temporal and other.

(There is no humbug so sedulously propagated as that regarding the *stupidity* of the business magnate. It is obvious why it is to that gentleman's advantage to have you believe that he is stupid. Such "stupid" business magnates do exist, no doubt. But there are, but too plainly, many who are not stupid at all. It is perhaps *safer* not to believe too implicitly in this much-advertised stupidity. I only throw out this suggestion. You are perfectly at liberty to disregard my caution.)

To run over now what I have been saying: Being a feminist, I believe that women should have freedom, so long as it is not destructive of non-feminine freedom: I like the negro, and think he should not be discriminated against. Again, men and women are usually more interesting at twenty than at forty. But all that has nothing to do with what I have been describing, and in no way impinges upon the accuracy of my analysis.

A "sex war," an "age war," a "color-line war," are all equally promoted by Big Business to cheapen labor and to enslave men more and more. I do not like the present capitalist system. It seems to me to be a very bad system indeed. I believe that it brings into anything it touches something destructive and evil. So, I think, we should learn to discriminate between some given humanitarian truth, upon the one hand, and that truth as destructively presented to us (as is generally the case) by the propaganda department of the great financial interest (namely the newspapers, or in books, films, etc.) upon the other.

Now Germany is the place where the youth-movement started. And today what the *Angriff* asserts is largely the truth—namely, that "The Youth-movement has become the Hitler-movement."

In the German Supplement to the *Times* in 1929 there was an interesting article upon German conditions today. The writer of that article regretfully confessed that the youth-movement was over: it had broken up, he said, into a series of separate political movements, attached to the various contending political parties. *Youth had become political!*

The Hitler Movement is a movement of young men and women. The Berlin leader of the Nazis, for instance, Dr. Goebbels, is thirty-four. And the rank and file of the movement show a preponderance of young men and young women. Half at least of the academic youth of Germany are supporters of Hitler. There are great numbers of young workmen in the movement, just as was the case with the Fascist movement at the start.

Now what is very peculiar is that when a leader like Hitler or Mussolini secures the support of the youth of the country, the press at once begins describing this misguided youth as *political cannon-fodder*. The Fascists, or the National Socialists, are *making use* of youth, for their own disgusting political ends! Were the same bodies of young men and young women following the Red Banner, they would look on very kindly and sigh, "Ah well. Boys will be Boys!" If these youngsters were attending Social Democratic "Youth-at the-Helm" rallies, they would be delighted!

I am not an advocate of Hitlerism, nor yet of Italian Fascism. But what is certain is that if you want to see youth at work and in its element—with all its characteristic passion and idealism—you cannot do better than go to the meetings of the Hitlerists. There "Youth-at-the-Helm" is not a phrase, but a fact, and youth with its eyes wide open! But that is not at all what is expected of youth by the golden-tongued, insinuating youth-fans. No—"*youth* has become so political!" they sigh. As though youth, in their sense, had ever been anything else but political! Youth-mysticism is purely political in origin (cf. the youth-mysticism in Fascist Italy or Russia). It will sound very strange to most English ears I know: but in fact "Young Woodley" is fundamentally just as political in its essential impulse as a speech by Winston Churchill. Art it is not, but it may be quite good politics. Far from being a romantic fact, youth has become a political fact. People only complain about this if they do not like the brand of politics involved.

PART V

"ALL THAT IS NOT RACE IN THIS WORLD IS DROSS"

BLUTSGEFÜHL

◆

"Was nicht Rasse ist auf dieser Welt, ist Spreu."[13]

Adolf Hitler, *Mein Kampf,* p. 313

Next I suggest that you earnestly grapple with the national Socialist doctrine of the *Blutsgefühl*. The whole bag of tricks of National Socialist theory is contained in that bloody portmanteau-word. I propose that we unpack it here and now, and ascertain pronto what the thing contains. And I do not disguise my belief that there is more in it than meets the eye. It is a rather difficult notion for the lackadaisical non-political mind of the Anglo-Saxon to get hold of. But I will do my best to make it pass into that particular intellectual receptacle "without tears," and I think I can guarantee to strip it of its for-the-English-or-American-repellant metaphysical attributes.

This dogma of the *Blutsgefühl,* or the blood-feeling, will lead us (for it is implicated with it) into the whole problem of nationalism. So in the next three chapters we shall perforce transcend the geographical limits of the particular dogmas of National Socialism, and find ourselves engaged in a consideration of the general principles that lie behind any such nationalist manifestation as Hitlerism.

To start with, I will quote a few lines from a typical article upon this subject (*Nationsozialistische Briefe*, November 15th, 1930):

> Der Nationalsozialismus predigt das Zeitalter des Blutes. Aus dem Blutsgefühl heraus soll sich ein neuer Wille zum Nationalismus und Sozialismus gebären, aus dem bewussten Blutsgefühl.

---

[13] "All that is not race in this world is dross."

Auch das Mittelalter lebt auf Grund der bluthaften Verbundenheit der Glieder des Volkes. Nur war diese bluthafte Verbundenheit nicht bewusst. Die Ethik des Mittelalters war christlich. Das Bluthaft-Metaphysische wurde unterdrückt auf Kosten des mönchischen Asketentums, das immer blutsverneinend wirkte, weil es eine nur auf Geist gesetzte Welt war. Der Körper wurde als Hindernis empfunden und verneint, die Pflege der bluthaften Eigenart als fl.eischliche Sünde abgetan.

Trotz allen dieser Massnahmen gegen den Instinkt des Blutes lebt er heute noch. Der Nationalsozialismus baut auf dieses Blutsgefühl auf.[14]

National Socialism is founded upon the blood-feeling: the Christian asceticism of the Middle-ages, this writer asserts, was always *blutsverneinend* or blood-denying—he appeals to a more pagan, and less metaphysical, reality. *The Instinct of the Blood*—the bodily poise, color, shape, and smell—that is to be the bond—but a bond based upon similarity, not upon difference. That profound race-sympathy is to be encouraged at all costs: likewise, the first instinctive revulsion to all that is strange, and belonging to a distinct and alien culture, must not be suppressed, it must be enthusiastically admitted to our consciousness and entertained.

National Socialism builds upon this blood-feeling! What Walt Whitman termed "the talk of the turning eyeballs"—it is that that you are required to understand. But whereas Walt Whitman (with

---

[14] "National Socialism teaches the Age of Blood. Out of the blood-feeling a new will to nationalism and to socialism shall be born. Out of the conscious blood-feeling.

"The Middle-ages also lived upon the basis of a blood-connection between the individual members of the race. Only then the blood-connection was not conscious. The tthic of the Middle-ages was Christian. The blood-metaphysic was suppressed because of the monkish asceticism, which always operated in a *blood-denying* sense, since theirs was a world established only upon mind. The body was felt to be a hindrance and denied—attention to blood-peculiarity stamped out as a sin of the flesh.

"In spite of all these measures against the blood-instinct, it is still alive today. National Socialism builds upon this blood-feeling."

his cosmic enthusiasms, his bursting and blatant romanticism, his lyrical cult of a universal brotherhood) sought to enlist this sort of fleshly second-sight in the service of *diffusion*, the present-day *Blutsgefühl* doctrinaires invoke it on behalf of a greater *concentratio*n. For the American nineteenth century prophet would have it employed to decipher "the talk of the turning eyeballs" in the heads of *whatever* man they revolved (provided he went upright and were certified a human being). But these newer Germanic blood-mystics invoke the human body to an end *opposite of that* of the great revolutionary sentimentalist and romantic—who had himself photographed for preference nude, and who called himself "Walt" and invited everybody else to do so.

What the doctrine of the *Blutsgefühl* aims at—as set down above in the passage quoted—is this. It desires a *closer and closer* drawing together of the people of one race and culture, by means of bodily attraction. It must be a true bodily solidarity. Identical rhythms in the arteries and muscles, and in the effective neural instrument-that should provide us with a passionate *exclusiveness*, with a homogeneous social framework, within the brotherly bounds of which we could live secure from alien interference, and so proceed with our work and with our pleasures, whatever they may be.

That is the big idea.

"*Damn braces, bless relaxes*!" shouted William Blake, who in many ways resembled Walt. The naked figures of Mr. and Mrs. Blake squatting in their suburban conservatory among the flower-pots playing at being Adam and Eve before the Fall, taken straight out of the puritan Bible, match very well the rhetorical nudity of Walt, genitals well to the fore in true patriarchal fashion, in the Atlantic surf upon the distant shores of the New World—the New Anglo-Saxony at that time.

But romantic cosmos-fans like Walt and Blake (and D.H. Lawrence was a tardy degenerate exemplar of this boisterous breed) are not only out-of-date in the merely fashionable sense, they are also out-of-date in the profounder sense that they are absolutely *mal-apropos*. *Historically* today they are on all sides confuted. Such a world as the present one could never spontaneously produce them, and it could have no possible use for them. And it is even, for all our sakes (as the stupidest of us must at last discover), a pity that such a type of person ever existed. For such promiscuous and expansive mystics, with their super-emotional appeals, prepared the way for the disintegration of our Western society. That society was a poor thing, but our own, and we surely would have improved it, if we had only known how to keep it intact.

Who, at all events, can deny that there is a great deal of political apropos and sagacity in the doctrine of these German nationalist leaders? It is their plan to *draw in* and to *concentrate*, rather than to diffuse, disperse and mix.

It is extremely easy to be facetious with regard to their "pure Germanism." "Aryan" is a useful word—it conveys something that is well-defined enough, for me at all events, but is ethnologically indefensible, I daresay. And I do not pretend myself to regard many of their dogmas in detail as acceptable. Still, there is, very much, another side to this humanitarian superior scorn about race, and the Anglo-Saxon should not be too complacent perhaps about the entire absence in himself of any feeling that could be described as racial. I am persuaded that the *opposite*—the diffusionist, racial-*olla-podrida* camp—is equally if not easier to ridicule. And personally, I advocate a great deal of such ridicule. I think it will have a good effect. You cannot laugh enough, it seems to me, at such a literary prophet as D.H. Lawrence, with his fetish of promiscuity and hysterical paeans to all that is "dark and strange."

So by *developing* (rather than *relaxing,* as happens in the Cosmopolitan West) the love and understanding of blood-brothers, of one culture, children of the same tradition, whose deepest social interest, when all is said and done, are one: that is the only sane and realistic policy in the midst of a disintegrating world. That, as I interpret it, is the National Socialist doctrine of the *Blutsgefühl*.

I have described above that expansive romanticism after the manner of Whitman, as being out-of-date. But there is one date, or time, for the Anglo-Saxon, it seems, and another for Europe. The sun reaches us later—but the intellectual dating is not an affair of clocks. It is difficult to say what it is. It was, at all events, of European time that I spoke.

Is it not true (if you are disposed to doubt what I have just said) that the English or American Undergraduate-and *á plus forte raison* the workmen and their native industrial-chiefs—are ignorant of any but those two far too over-simple alternatives—namely an unadulterated Toryism, upon the one hand, and an unadulterated communism upon the other? If in Anglo-Saxony an undergraduate would be very bright and advanced politically, he speaks in cordial terms of Moscow and the Russians, or if he is really a proper devil, he simply joins the Communist Party. If on the other hand he inclines to say, "I am old-fashioned perhaps, but, etc."—then there is nothing for him but an old and crusted Toryism. There is *nothing outside* these two far too over-simple things. The enlightened mind of Anglo-Saxony simply does not function anywhere *between*, or *outside*, those two fixed, conventional landmarks. And that is as good as to say, of course (seeing all we have seen, in one direction and another, since 1914), that it does not function *at all*. It is beyond question the idlest, most stationary, out-of-date, mental machine in the world today. And the young American undergraduate who looks for guidance to Mr. Kurstein, and listens to his veiledly communizing "*Tally-ho*," is no better than that Young England who, in Cambridge, suffers Mr. Brownowski to be its guide, philosopher, and friend.

So how extremely the opposite such a doctrine as I have been outlining above is to all that we are accustomed to in the

Anglo-Saxon, the pure Western, world, I scarcely need to point out. Here we are all of us, in one shape or another, *exoticists*. The only thing that has any advertisement-value is what is *different* from what we are—what is strange—and so (here enters the social-snobbery) amusing. For we are all very much our little gentleman, and would go into fits of giggles or discreet "ha-ha's" at that German seriousness, oh yes! which looks behind the conventional political facades, and rummages at the foundations of all political doctrines.

But in England especially we have suffered, for a century, from a perfect frenzy of *exoticism*. We have tasted, breathed, and thought the exotic. And it has been a drug, with the stupid intoxication of its perfume, that has at last thoroughly enervated our minds.

With the early nineteenth century romantics (the children of Rousseauism and the French Revolution) every refinement of exoticism came into vogue. All the celebrated English poets of that time—the Byrons and Shelleys—were both noisy, picturesque and empty humanitarian revolutionaries, and at the same time worshippers of the strange. The great French poets of the nineteenth century were the same. Charles Baudelaire made a point of having an enormous mulatto mistress. Rimbaud went to Africa to live. Later on, the romantic painter Gauguin went to the South Seas, and enjoyed a very great vogue with his rather sugary fakes of the pictorial art of Polynesia.

Today Paul Gauguin is totally discredited as an artist—I pity anybody attempting to auction a Gauguin picture at the present time. It is very unlikely that there will be any swing of the pendulum, either, in favor of such pictures. Indeed, all that description of exotic *geographical* romanticism is eclipsed, as far as the world of serious criticism, or of the most serious art, is concerned. It has died a violent death at the hands of the new men that the dramatic times we live in have rapidly bred up. It survives only in such superficial bookstall-literature as that of Paul Morand

(*Bouddha Vivant*, *Magie Noire*, etc.). This I think we may all agree is an extremely good thing. I say we may agree, but do we in fact agree? For do we *act upon* our newer and profounder critical values? Do we not rather just affect those values (in order to be up-to-date) and then stagnate?

The heavily-scented, old, exoticism lingers still among the moneyed amateur art-students, of course. There are always a few rich high-brow tourists and super-studio-tenants, big game-hunters, film stars, executant musicians, and American society-women who wish to demonstrate how staggeringly original they can be (how broad-minded and un-babbitty). The latter do still in the province of New York, I believe (oh horror of horrors!), go to bed with a negro—who it is to be hoped, stout fellow, laughs at them with a hyena-whoop of hysterical black-laughter from time to time up his sleeve. There is too, of course, still the D.H. Lawrence vogue—it languishes, but it lives on. And Lawrence was chock-full of a most enraged exoticism—it dripped in aromatic drops from his pages. When he painted pictures in oils, he produced, as one might have expected, a quantity of inferior Gauguins. But the exotic sense, which is at the very heart of the romantic temper, is in a moribund condition today beyond question.

In connection with the doctrine of the *Blutsgefühl*, it would be very useful, I think, if we subjected the exotic sense to a brief analysis. The romantic, luxurious sensationalism that caused Charles Baudelaire to acquire a mulatto mistress, and that enables the theatrical, musical and other impresarios to put over all the negro-stuff that literally swamps America at this minute, deserves far more attention than I can give it here. In my next chapter I will however supply an analysis that may be some slight corrective to the usual sentimental opiate.

ANALYSIS OF THE EXOTIC SENSE
───◆───

I will now provide, in order to arrive at a clearer understanding of the problems involved in the National Socialist doctrine of the *Blutsgefühl*, a rough analysis of the exotic sense. For it is the irresponsible operations of that par excellence *romantic* sensibility which chiefly inhibits the sane functioning of that other, deeper understanding. Indeed, it is precisely an egotistic, destructive, slighting of that feeling that is the first step towards the other sensation: or it is only that that makes it possible at all.

But first of all, the exotic sense implies a self-repudiation, too. It is a delicious suicide of the group-soul in us—this romantic abandonment to the strange, for strangeness' sake. The exotic sense, in the nature of things, is a direction taken by the mind that implies decadence. For it is a flight from the self, is it not—a yearning for violent change? No very active man could experience it—he would be too absorbed with the satisfactions of his own personal activity to wish to transfer his attentions so far away from his vital and effective center—his own creative principle of life. Essentially it is non-creative: it possesses the characteristics of the traditional feminine surrender, rather than of the male insurgence and egoism.

At its heart, it can be nothing but a pathetic diffusive expansion towards some otherness, which will, it is felt, satisfy, where the thing-we-know does not. The ego is discredited, when such a state of mind exists as causes the individual to fling himself at the feet of one alien ego after another, in flight from his own, in a feverish centrifugalism.

It is not surprising therefore to find that the exotic sense flourishes above all in what we term a period of "decadence." It is a defeatism, concerned as it is with the native values we inherit. In its result, it provides for a superficial assimilative existence, passed as sampler, or taster, of things we can never make our own.

But there is a further condition, which it is most important to note in connection with this pseudo-artistic appetite for the not-self as such: namely, that all indulgence in the exotic sense postulates a state of affairs in which the person indulging in it belongs to a social system still powerful and superior in its resources to the system to which the object of the exoticist's infatuation belongs. That is essential. It is an aristocratic, or a plutocratic, indulgence—of the same order as globe-trotting, or big-game-hunting, or foreign missionary work.

In the mid-nineteenth century the white races of Western Europe had overrun the earth, communist disintegration was not yet in existence, the Western supremacy was unchallenged. But the period of expansion, and that of easy money, and lightly won power, had drawn to a close. Anglo-Indian colonels' trousers were worshipped, shrines built for their reception, by superstitious natives, astounded at the spectacle of the white man's power. And the white overlord began to get a little soft and to let himself go a little bit. The moment was ripe for the appearance of the exoticist upon the scene! What after all is the exoticist, but the White conqueror turned literary and sentimental?

It is really advisable to see these things a little clearly. Thus, it has *not* been the Borneo headhunter who studied *us*: it was we who went out and indulged in the pleasures of anthropological research at his expense. The Mexican peon did *not* get romantic (to come down to the present time) about Mr. D.H. Lawrence. It was Mr. D.H. Lawrence who got a lot of romantic, self-indulgent, satisfaction out of contemplation of the Mexican peon. But had Mr. D.H. Lawrence gone to Mexico five hundred years ago, attracted by the marvelous romance of the plumed serpent-god, then Mr. Lawrence would immediately have been pole-axed and popped into the sacrificial pot for the god's breakfast at sunrise the next morning.

But here we arrive at this still more central fact. Mr. D.H.

Lawrence, five hundred years ago, would have been a Cortes—or nothing. And in that case, he would have been too busy defending his own white skin to have had either time or inclination to swoon at the beauty of the Mexican Indian's greasy copper integument. Also, upon the positive side, his pleasures and satisfactions would have been of a very different order. They would as a matter of fact have been more real. He would have been exercising all his wits and sinews (if successful, to his enormous personal satisfaction no doubt)—in getting the better—that is, conquering—this copper-skinned ant-heap, sunk in its stupid blood-rites. And he would have sent up an old Spanish, or old English, or monk-Latin prayer to the Hebrew god of battle, in gratefulness for the fell work of his men's up-to-date blunderbusses.

That, in a rather grotesque nutshell, is the rock-bottom commonsense of this rather dismal exotic sense, is it not? It has been an unexampled pest in the latter-day European democratic societies; still yearly it takes its toll, in a hundred different ways, of our failing political might-of all those advantages, in short, which have made civilized life possible to us.

A very great European, Cervantes in fact, said all this a long time ago; and *Don Quixote* contains the same order of criticism of the unpractical, dreamy, European in which I am engaged in this essay, and over which I have spent so much time in other essays.

What is the American fashion of negro-worship, with its basis in the jazz-cult, but an exotic sense operating on the spot, as it were? For the American does not have to make long journeys to the Congo or the Zambezi to have his black exotic thrill. There are all the blacks, browns, and high yallers that the most exotic heart can desire at his own front door, or peeling potatoes in his back kitchen.

But does it not indicate a serious misunderstanding of his own world-position (this I ask under correction and with no desire to offend) that the American should let himself go to this extent? Is it not conceited, over-sanguine, even pretentious, as well as very unreflective of him? Can he, in fact, politically *afford* to admit these more and more "romantic" fifteen million black pets to his big star-spangled bosom? For, delightful as the negroes are—in some respects no doubt more cheerful, musical and light-hearted folks than the whites—yet they are only human. Give them all your jobs, exalt them much above your own Babbitt-hood, and (being but human) they will surely take advantage of this heaven-sent reversal of status. And *they* will not then find the poor white trash by whom they are surrounded anything like so "romantic" and bewitching as the white American has been persuaded, cajoled, and bullied into finding *them*. The American negro, once in power, would probably not be very much troubled by the exotic sense!

What is the upshot of all this, then? Why, I can see nothing for it, I am bound to confess, but to put the following disobliging question to the Western European, and (with more diffidence) to the American: "When, sir, when, madam, are you going to stop *playing*? The self-indulgent nineteenth century white playboy is today historically nonsense. When, oh when do you propose to put away childish things then—for you are, in the post-war world of debt and dole, no longer in the position of a spoiled child? When are you going to realize, do you suppose, how things have altered for all of us? It would be nice to know! When do you think we may expect you to draw in your horns, to face the fact that you are no longer a white overlord or anything jolly of that sort at all, and to give your best attention to the safeguarding of your famous white skin, and as a consequence cease sentimentalizing with regard to the non-white world, of whatever hue or kind?"

To this the Hitlerist would add: "When, respected sir, and gracious lady, are you going—oh short-sighted, much-indulging, sentimentally-renegade person that you are!—when may we hope that you will turn for a change to more practical interests? How about giving your white consciousness a try for a little—it is really not so dull as you suppose! A white Australia—that may be impracticable. But at least there is nothing impracticable about a white Europe. And today Europe is not so big as it was. It is 'a little peninsula at the Western extremity of Asia.' It is quite small. Why not all of us draw together, and put our white civilization in a state of defense? And let us start by mutually cancelling all these monstrous debts that are crushing the life out of us economically."

In arguments regarding the classical in contrast to the romantic temper, it is generally conceded that there is nothing that defines the classical outlook so much as a capacity to find interest in what is under your nose, rather than what is remote and strange. And it does undoubtedly require far more imagination to take an interest in an object (person or thing) to which you are used, than in one that you see for the first time (in something that is outlandish, queer, amusing, mysterious and therefore dark, strange and surprising).

The greatest civilizations (those of China, Egypt, or India) have been very exclusive indeed. In the supreme moment of action, the Western countries, in their struggle with the rest of the world, were exclusive, too, and Christian only in name, certainly not in deed. Should not they at present become exclusive once more?

The doctrine of the *Blutsgefühl* is a violent affirmation of the political beliefs which I have just outlined.

One of the most interesting episodes in the war-literature of the last half-decade is to be found, it seems to me, in a story by Captain Herbert Read, M.C. The hero has brought in a German officer, made prisoner by him after a pistol-duel in No Man's Land. The German is brought down to Battalion-Headquarters: there our hero leaves him for a few minutes, being called away to attend to something outside. Upon his return he finds that a considerable disturbance is in progress. His German prisoner, under guard, is violently denouncing, from the opening of the dugout, the English officers present—*all* the English, as a matter of fact—for their "race-treachery," as he calls it. That German prisoner for me was a better man, and he had something more intelligible to utter, than most of the famous figures of war-literature.

These at all events are beliefs—and we can conveniently classify them under the title of the doctrine of the *Blutsgefühl*—that are very prevalent among all educated Germans. Such a way of feeling has caused them to resist the jazz-culture and a hundred other things, in a manner that would have been quite impossible in an Anglo-Saxon country. But can we any longer deny that that German belief in the necessity of a central, Western, unified culture, and the necessity of a acute and more jingoistic, if you like, race-consciousness on the part of all white Western peoples, has something to be said for it?

This is not a sentimental issue at all. Do not allow yourself to be hoodwinked into believing that by its opponents. On the contrary, it is a severely practical one. The political and economic structure of Western Europe and of America are in a state of violent disequilibrium. Something has to be done of a most radical sort; very rapidly indeed, it seems. And I suggest that the sort of solution indicated in Hitlerism is not entirely to be despised, though not necessarily to be swallowed whole.

The Fox and the Goose

I will go to the fountainhead of Hitlerism, namely, the writings of Hitler. The eleventh chapter of his book, *Mein Kampf*, is entitled *Volk und Rasse*. And it begins in the zoological garden of nature, as it were, and, in true peasant style, he goes to the Fox and the Goose, the Cat and the Finch, for worldly instruction.

He starts by saying that there are many truths that are so obvious that they escape everybody's notice: and then he directs your attention to the particular pragmatic truth that he is here concerned with—namely, the *exclusiveness* of nature, in respect of the various life-forms to be found in the animal creation. "Every animal pairs exclusively with a mate of the same species as itself." If it does otherwise, nature registers her protest by causing her offspring to be barren, or else by robbing them of *Widerstandsfähigkeit*, against sickness or enemy attack.

"The Fox is always a Fox," he says. "*Der Fuchs ist immer ein Fuchs, die Gans eine Gans, der Tiger ein Tiger, u. s. w.*" And he ends this passage with the remark:

> Es wird aber nie ein Fuchs zu finden sein, der seiner inneren Gesinnung nach etwa humane Anwandlungen Gansen gegenüber haben könnte, wie es ebenso auch keine Katze gibt mit freundlicher Zuneigung zu Mäusen.[15]

We are reminded of William Blake's "The Lion never lost so much time as when he consented to learn of the Fox."

Whither this reasoning is intended to conduct us, it is obvious, is to a sense of the danger inherent in the drying-up or the blunting

---

[15] "No fox will ever be found possessed of a fancy after the human manner with regard to a goose, just as likewise no cat exists with a friendly inclination towards mice."

of our primitive instincts, which permits us to mate with people of an inferior race. (Racial inferiority and superiority is taken for granted almost. In any case, "I am superior to you" is the instinctive attitude of any living organism.) Such a bastardization is race-suicide (for nature will rapidly revenge herself upon us)—even though it may be, certainly, in some cases, for the *individual*, something like the enjoyment of a maggoty cheese—much better fun than homely cheddar! And this is not a moral consideration at all: it is a purely practical one. Race-loyalty is one of the elementary conditions of self-security and of self-survival.

So far so good. What, first of all, is to be noticed in these arguments, is that the animals contrasted are the beast of prey and its victim—the fox and the farmyard goose, the cat and the mouse. The reason why nature does not like her elaborately evolved species to mix, is because the *better* would then inevitably be mixing with the *worse*—not the craft of the fox, for instance, with the fronton bravery of the lion. Efficiency would diminish. Why the donkey may not with impunity mate with the horse, is because the latter is the *nobler* animal, apparently.

There is a difficulty here: for we are inclined to ask whether there is anything ultimately more desirable in being a horse rather than in being a donkey. On the face of it, a racehorse would be a jollier thing to be, it is true, than any ass that ever brayed. If it really came to the point, most of us given the choice would find ourselves in a racing-stable rather than chewing a turnip. Yet there is always something to be said for the donkey. It might even be the philosopher's choice. But it would never be the man-of-action's.

Really the point is, I think, that we "Aryans," or whatever we are, are faced with extinction. We cannot afford just now to be philosophers, nor yet humanitarians. No one will be philosophical, nor yet humanitarian, with *us*. Yes, the above argument of Hitler's is an argument for *an emergency*. Everything now almost, since the War, seems a matter of life and death. It is not an argument for the scientific mind, but for the political mind.

As such this perhaps prejudiced zoology has considerable meaning. I do not write this book *from choice*, for; instance: I would far rather, if it rested with me, be engaged in scientific research, or in artistic creation. Ever since in the War, where I served on the Western Front with the artillery, I was first under fire, there are certain questions I have asked of life which it would never have occurred to me to ask before. The War, as you are aware, went on and on, and these questions in the end *asked themselves* as it were, with a more obstinate urgency every day. Nothing had warned me, prior to that, to expect such great number of shells, bullets, and bombs to rain suddenly out of nothingness, all aimed essentially at *my* head (the shells for which I, on my side, was responsible, went into nothingness. I saw nothing, but doubtless far away their explosions provoked a similar mood to mine).

A state of emergency came to appear for me, as for most soldiers, a permanent thing. Unlike, I daresay, most of my companions, I realized that something in this "storm of steel" required explaining: and the academic meteorology of average public opinion, or of the press, for these monstrous disturbances, was unsatisfactory. And since that time, it is naturally easier to convince me of the imminence of such a condition or of its being a condition inherent in the very nature of our life.

Some soldiers, it is true, kept smiling throughout this tempest of steel; some also who survived write war-books in which the cheerio-spirit is still to the fore—the "humor" fed out to the Tommy, to protect him from his own thoughts, and to protect (from him) those responsible for his misery. But I, figuratively, have never smiled again. At all events, I have never grinned to order—this will explain what I mean by "emergency," I hope.

So, under the compulsion of such emergency conditions, values change, and we are forced to admit arguments which, in other circumstances, we might regard as unsound. In brief, we are

"ALL THAT IS NOT RACE IN THIS WORLD IS DROSS"

compelled, I think, to lay more stress upon what is pragmatic and *useful*, and less upon what is perhaps eternally true. It is a case of *force majeure*. I surrender, therefore, to the argument of the Fox and the Goose, the Cat and the Mouse. We are in the greatest danger. Gentleness, beauty, sweet reason must veil their heads, they must give way to arguments of *power*.

As a *power-argument* (and it of course is essentially as a power-argument that Hitler, a very intelligent man, presents it) the above zoological parallel is a good one. "Wer leben will, der kämpfe also," Hitler says, "und wer nicht streiten will in dieser Welt des ewigen Ringens, verdient das Leben nicht."[16] That is the simple statement of the Darwinian-Nietzschean struggle for existence. So long as by "struggle" here is meant *intelligent struggle*, today such sentiments are unimpeachable: so long as it is remembered that the whole of Napoleon's Old Guard could be wiped out with a spot of poison-gas, that the splendid Prussian regiments which caused Nietzsche so much impulsive pride could be exterminated by a bombing plane or two—in short, that the old German warrior-nation is out-of-date—that the battle is to the cunning and not any longer to the strong. Still, the spirit of the "Youth of Langemarck" is not to be despised. And in civil war it is more valuable than in real war.

Hitler is a man-of-action: but action for him is, a little, compulsory action—it is not action-for-action's sake altogether. So he says (*Mein Kampf*, p. 304):

Tatsächlich ist die pazifistisch-humane Idee vielleicht ganz gut dann, wenn der höchststehende Mensch sich vorher die Welt

---

[16] "So if you want to live, you fight," Hitler says, "and if you do not want to fight in this world of eternal struggle, you do not deserve life."

erobert und unterworfen hat in einem Umfange, der ihn zum alleinigen Herrn dieser Erde macht.[17]

In other words, if you were master of the earth, *then* it would be all right to harbor humanitarian beliefs. *Pax Romana* is the only reasonable pacifism!—"Also erst Kampf, und dann kann man sehen, was zu machen ist."[18] Emergency-doctrine, again!

---

[17] "In fact, the pacifist-humane idea may be quite good if the highest human being has previously conquered and subdued the world to the extent that he is the sole master of this Earth."
[18] "So fight first, and then you will see what to do."

"Aryanism" in Politics, and "Diffusionism" in Anthropology

—◆—

Of course, once you have surrendered to the Fox and Goose argument, the rest is easy. All the same, it will be better to consider what comes next, and to admit at once all the difficulties that are to be encountered in this variety of the "Blonde Beast" theory.

For all that we admire upon this earth at present, one *race* is probably responsible, says Adolf Hitler:

> Alles, was wir heute auf dieser Erde bewundern—Wissenschaft und Kunst, Technik und Erfindungen—ist nur das schöpferische Produkt weniger Völker und vielleicht ursprünglich einer Rasse. Von ihnen hängt auch der Bestand dieser ganzen Kultur ab. Gehen sie zugrunde, so sinkt mit ihnen die Schönheit dieser Erde in das Grab.[19]

This great creative race, which is responsible for all the technical, artistic, and cultural achievements of civilized life, is the Aryan— all that we see is "nahezu ausschliesslich schöpferisches Produkt des Ariers."[20] If this race quitted, then for good and all "die menschliche Kultur würde vergehen und die Welt veroöden."[21]

Now the so-called "diffusionist school" of anthropologists in England, of which Professor Elliot Smith is the principal representative, believes the same thing. Only it is not the Aryans that the latter have picked for this role—Professor Elliot Smith is

---

[19] "Everything that we admire on this Earth today—science and art, technology and inventions—is only the creative product of fewer people and perhaps originally of a race. The existence of this entire culture also depends on them. If they perish, the beauty of this Earth sinks into the grave with them."
[20] "Almost exclusively Aryan creative product"
[21] "human culture would pass away and the world would be ruined."

persuaded that it is the Egyptian which is the genius amongst races. What is of some interest, however, in the present connection, is the nature of the arguments of the English diffusionists. For they contend that most races show no trace of inventive energy whatever, and that, if left to themselves, they would never progress beyond a very modest level of stagnant barbarity. They insist that *spontaneous* outbursts of creative and inventive energy (from all we know of the majority of primitive communities, and for that matter, of mankind in general) is not to be looked for. Indeed, it is so unlikely, that we are compelled to find some other reason for the wide dispersal of civilized conditions of life. Civilization, they argue, must have been diffused throughout the world from some one creative source of energy, and it was probably the invention of a single race or community.

They also say (on behalf of their solitary and unique creative race) that, as time passes, this culture irradiated from an ancient source of intellectual light, gets thinner and thinner. With the Romans a great mass of this treasure of enlightenment was lost or coarsened. We ourselves are dissipating still more of it. At length nothing will be left.

So the diffusionist school of anthropologists think as the Hitlerist does—namely, that there is *something*, the monopoly of a single race, which, when it disappears, will leave mankind plunged once more in a Dark Age of semi-animal eclipse. Since the original gift of civilization was an accident that is unlikely to recur, the primitive darkness would then doubtless be permanent.

In this respect at least the Aryan School in politics, and the diffusionist school of anthropology, are at one.

When we consider the intellectual darkness of Africa (with the exception of the Nile Valley)—the similar unresourcefulness of the negritic south of India, the absolutely stationary condition of the Australian aborigine (in whom, because of his isolation, it is suggested, we have a paradigm of average humanity, when left to its own devices)—there is something to be said for the European—the Aryan—Whites—those people who in the remote past brought civilization to India, and possibly to Chaldea and to China too. It appears that any such notion must remain the merest speculation, for too little information so far is available, we are told, to do more than guess. All I am suggesting is that it is not in itself a *ridiculous* notion, as it is too much the habit—in the anti-Aryan West—to assert.

It was the mathematical-inventiveness of the (presumably white) Hindu, that was responsible for Arabian Mathematics, and, it is quite likely, of those of Greece. And the most ancient tradition of the Hindus tells of *another country*, from which they (the first civilized men in India) had come: and the tradition in every case points to a colder land than the Indian. And the records of the earliest civilization in Mesopotamia, before the Semitic Empires, seems to suggest possibilities of something favorable to the Aryan theorist.

These are the order of things upon which this race-theory is based, and it is necessary to recapitulate them in order to be able to talk about such a theory as Aryanism at all. In short, it is necessary to remember that the Aryan *white-hope* notion is not simply idiotic, although it is speculative. It would only be idiotic if you considered it idiotic to wish the particular race to which you belong to be the inventor of civilization. And I do find it difficult to see why that should be so idiotic, even if you say that it does not matter so much as all that.

Doughty, in his *Arabia Deserta*, was very emphatic about the unbelievable mechanical uninventiveness of the Arab. They are incapable, he says, of conceiving the most elementary mechanical improvement, or undertaking the simplest technical repairs, sanitary or other. And at least no one will dispute that the European has been the star-technician of the world, though Greece and Italy are, in the first place, Europe, in that connection.

To return to Hitler, however: when, as a politician and

therefore propagandist, he says that all the science and Art, technique and invention in the world is the work of the White European, or Aryan, one must agree as to the technique of material progress—of mechanical inventiveness—but as to art it would be very easy to demur. And art is a great factor, in the modern world, in the power-situation. Politically, far more is done by masses and masses of newspaper articles, than by straight reasoning or by big battalions. This knack for idiotic verbiage is not *art*, it is quite true, but there is a sort of rudimentary and vulgar art-instinct present.

Film-plays, books, cartoons, and so on, are of the first importance in bringing about such a state of mind as is desired by the political interests financing those activities. And for all those things the Aryan has an inferior gift (of which, seeing their quality, he need not be very ashamed): he is far less good at them than are other people. Still, in matters of the technique of art, as opposed to the technique of science, and at this in fields where a great deal of taste and intelligence is required, the Hitlerist's arch-enemy, the Jew, can make rings round him in all that universe that is not war, or mechanical technique. It seems to me that, even from an Aryan standpoint, it is essential to concede such patent facts as these, in order that we may realize the handicap. Aryan, and especially German, clumsiness in the technique of art, should be faced—if only that it may be overcome. Again, no Aryan mathematician has succeeded in putting Einstein in his place: indeed, all the Aryan mathematicians of Europe follow him like obedient mooing cattle—perhaps, if one knew more about it, *too much* like cattle. Still there it is—such facts do seem to circumscribe Herr Hitler's boast, and in some respects to negative it.

Reduced to technique—to the mastery over matter—the Aryan claim does not appear so lofty as in the sweeping generalization we have read above. Are there perhaps two sorts of men, after all, who are the complement of one another, one is inclined to ask— men of action, and men of art, for instance? Is the present-day Aryan, in isolation, not enough? Without him, indeed, the civilized world might well go down (by reason of the valuable starch secreted in his character in great quantities). But is this Master of Matter not so superior after all as he has believed himself to be?

These are the arguments *against* Hitler's super-racial creed. Each man must answer them in his own way. Hitler himself remarks: "Nicht in den intellektuellen Gaben liegt die Ursache der kulturbildenden und aufbauenden Fähigkeit des Ariers."[22]

What he would no doubt reply to the qualifications set out above, regarding the cultural monopoly of the Aryan in the matter of art, at least, is this. He would say that no really great inventive genius has come from among the non-Aryan (he would mention the Jewish first) technicians of Europe: the Michelangelos, Sebastian Bachs, the Leonardos, and so on, were of the great life-giving white Aryan stock.

What, to sum up, I should say, is that the Aryan claim should be advanced in rather a different form to that made use of by the Hitlerist. The moment you take in the great Italian masters (or the Greek, "El Greco") you require a wider interpretation of Aryan: so wide, indeed, as to endanger this ideology altogether. But the remainder of what I have to say can best be dealt with in a separate chapter.

---

[22] "It is not the intellectual gifts that are the cause of the Aryan's ability to build and develop culture."

Aryan Hegemony and a Germanic *Volapuk*?

The Aryan notion, as an engine of political propaganda, the moment we begin scrutinizing it at all closely, entices us far beyond the political frontiers of any given nationality. Therein lies the difficulty. For that matter, when we begin talking of the "blood-feeling," and saying that we desire to isolate and to glorify that, we run head-on into the rather unreal modern conception of the nation at once—the Austrian nation, for instance—the Breton, the Irish, the Basque, the Swiss, the Ukrainian, *nation*. And, as will I think be seen, it is none too easy to reconcile a nationalist dogma of *Blutsgefühl* with a nationalist dogma of the nation.

I will endeavor to arouse the attention of the reader to the various important problems involved in all nationalist ideology—whether it be Irish, German, Polish, Catalonian, or Italian. German nationalism, in common with all the other nationalisms, has fundamentally the same objections to meet. And one of the interesting things about the present situation in Germany—it will provide the true test of the intelligence of its leaders—is just how the nationalist, and especially the National Socialist, movement, will deal with these inherent contradictions and practical obstacles.

It is an easy matter to get some sort of "blood-feeling" going where people speaking the same tongue are in question, living within defined historical frontiers. But it would be far more difficult to make the average Shetlander see that he is a pure blood brother of a Bavarian or a Breton. Indeed, if this were ever accomplished, it would be for the first time in history. *It would be a novel event, of the first magnitude.* That is no reason at all why it should not occur. All I am saying is that it would be a very great novelty.

Yet, language apart, it is really extraordinary how *identical* in personal appearance, essential habits of thought, instinctive mental reactions, and so forth, many Scots, Swiss, Bavarians, Bretons, Normans, Scandinavians, Austrians, and even Northern Italians, and Northern Spaniards, are. The *true* political solidarity should be between these kindred peoples—in *that* there would be some sense. In *nations* there is almost none. But language, and conventional national frontiers, cut across these far more logical and potent realities. How are you ever going to convey to these dispersed units of the same distinguished family (each jabbering a different speech) that they are cutting their own throats by cutting each other's? *The Great War was, in fact, a Great Civil War*. How can that be made clear to the majority? Will the press help us? No.

Far the greater number of Irish People are of good old Norse stock, and actually look as like as two peas, when closely compared, with the inhabitants, say, of Bristol—formerly sister-city to Dublin. (As late as the thirteenth century, Bristol and Dublin spoke the same Nordic, non-Celtic tongue, I believe I am right in saying.) Yet all that a Spanish (or is it Maltese) gentleman, Mr. De Valera, has to do is to come and strike some sad sobbing notes out of the Irish harp, and to howl in a melodious, carefully-cultivated brogue, about "Ould Ireland"—and the trick is done! These blood-brothers are at each other's throats—they fall upon each other like cat and dog! And a few bold, shrewdly aimed blows upon the Welsh harp, with a wild wail or two—that would have just the same effect! As to the bagpipes—if *they* were brought into play it is impossible to foresee what would happen! "*My sakes!*" as Mr. Bekins would say.

I feel that this part of my account of Hitlerism may fall short of what I should wish, and may sound too much like criticism, instead of just the work of a detached exponent. It is however because of my sympathy with this great German party, that I am concerned to see these difficulties brought out into the light, and, it is to be hoped, overcome.

The Hitlerist speaks confidently of "converting the world." By this is meant, I conclude, the Aryan world. "All that is not race is dross!" Herr Hitler cries. But race—not being identical with nation—as no one better than Hitler knows, born as he was a few miles outside the frontiers of Germany—how is this new solidarity to be managed? The mention of *one language*—a *Volapuk*—for Europe, the Hitlerist would regard with suspicion. Let it be a Germanic *Volapuk*, I would say then!

The Hitler Movement has done wonders inside the frontiers of Germany, and its leaders should, I think, extend their message—which also would be a message of peace—to other countries of a similar culture. They are, as Dr. Benes said, at the *center* of Europe. It is to them that we must look for a great movement of political *concentration*—to call a halt to the growing stagnation and diffusion elsewhere.

PART VI
HITLERIST ECONOMICS

WAR-DEBTS—AND THE GREAT CREDITOR-NATION, AMERICA

Hitler already wrote the sentence in his book *Mein Kampf* in 1924: "The struggle against international finance and loan capital has become the most important program item, the struggle of the German nation for its independence and freedom." *(Adolf Hitler's Goals and Personality, by Dr. Johannes Stark. Nobel Prize winner & University Professor).*

What more than anything else has directed the attention of the rest of the world to the Hitler Movement in Germany, is the Hitlerist attitude to *war debts*. The first great agitation there was organized by Hugenberg, the newspaper magnate and industrialist. The fact that this great capitalist identified himself with the advocates of debt-repudiation and found himself in the opposite camp to international finance, is highly suggestive. And immediately this conducts us to the heart of the economic doctrine of the National Socialist—namely, the absolute distinction between concrete and *productive* capital (great or small) upon the one hand, and loan-capital (as the Hitlerist calls it) upon the other. The arch-enemy is not *Das Kapital* pure and simple, as with Marx, but *Das Leihkapital*, or loan-capital. *Property*—up to some specified, reasonable, amount—the Hitlerist has no objection to. If you own a cow, that is all right. But if you have lent another money with which to buy a cow (probably at crushing interest-rates, and upon such terms as preclude the cow ever paying, as a cow, or being of any use to anybody except the loaner), and if you make a habit of lending people money to buy objects like cows—or cars, or cart-horses—that is quite another matter. At all that I will arrive, however, later.

So Hugenberg, the nationalist leader and industrialist, conducted a first-class political campaign against the *Erfühlungspolitik*, or policy of "understanding" and "fulfillment of obligations." The conditions imposed upon Germany by the Young Plan—the "Young Tribute"—could not be carried out, he said. Germany should simply repudiate this gigantic and unreasonable burden imposed upon her at the dictated peace of Versailles.

The Hitler Movement was of the same opinion as Hugenberg, only more so. And that movement has carried farther than he, with much greater success, this agitation. *Debts* are in short at the root of the whole success of Hitlerism in Germany. And it is because the Hitler Movement has been known first and foremost to stand for *debt* repudiation that it attracted the attention of the entire world. For upon definite *debt-repudiation* by Germany a world-wide upheaval would ensue.

In every country except the United States of America, moreover, this debt-nightmare is a very actual thing. The American has been the most unpopular figure in the post-War world because he was regarded as the prime cause of all the misery that ensued upon the Peace of Versailles—as the callous arch-creditor, the supreme Shylock. And even today *Amerikaner* is a word that brings hostility and disgust into the face of the German man-in-the-street.

That this picture of the American is false (if by "America" you mean the great mass of Americans—the American man-in-the-street) should by this time be patent to all Europeans. Indeed, it was never true, I should think, unless it were intended to refer to the money-barons of Wall Street. But there are money-Barons after all everywhere—America has no monopoly of them.

It may even be worthwhile to bring this home to people. I think I will just reproduce here a cutting from the *Times* of this morning's date (January 5th, 1931): and at the same time a cutting from the *Daily Telegraph* (also January 5th, 1931) describing bread-lines and the state of advanced distress in New York City. Here is the first of these documents, and on the next page you will find the second:

FARMERS' RIOT IN ARKANSAS
DEMAND FOR BREAD AND WORK
From our own Correspondent

The business district of the town of England, Arkansas, was last night stormed by over 500 farmers, ruined by drought and falling prices, who came in from the cotton and maize fields of Lonoke County, shouting "for bread and work," and threatening to loot the shops of the town unless they and their children were fed.

Mr. George Morris, a local lawyer who tried to pacify them, was howled down by the farmers, who shouted, "We want food, and we want it now. Our children are crying for food, and we are going to get it. Give us work and we will not come back." One man, pushing his way to the front of the crowd, told the lawyer that the farmers were willing to work for as little as 50 cents a day (2s.), but would not starve or let their families starve.

In the meantime the shopkeepers—themselves in an impoverished condition owing to the agricultural depression and the failure of the local bank—realizing that looting was likely to begin, held a conference and agreed to telephone to the Red Cross authorities at Little Rock, asking for authority to distribute food. The Red Cross, which is already feeding 100,000 people in the State, authorized the shopkeepers to give food on behalf of the Red Cross to the value of $2.75 cents (11s.) per family. With the appearance of these supplies the crowd became quieter and dispersed for the time being, but Mr. Morris said last night that they would undoubtedly return as soon as their supplies were exhausted. "The merchants of England," he said, "must either move their goods or mount machine-guns on their stores."

Representatives of the Red Cross at Little Rock said that they feared that the outbreak at England was only the prelude to further disturbances elsewhere in the state. The farmers of Lonoke

County were formerly fairly prosperous, but drought accompanied by a heavy fall in the prices of agricultural products have reduced them to penury. A similar situation exists all through Arkansas and the cotton country of Northern Texas and Southern Oklahoma, where a spirit of radicalism among the farmers, many of whom have lost their independence through inability to pay interest on mortgaged farms, has been growing rapidly since the summer. In a speech at the University of Virginia last summer Mr. Carl Williams, a member of the Federal Farm Board, and himself from that district, warned his hearers that a failure of effective remedies for the agricultural situation would be followed by violence and bloodshed.

Among these five hundred farmers it is very likely that many belong to the original white emigrant stock of the earliest colonists. Yet they are starving, and are ready to work for fifty cents a day to feed their families. No pioneer, faced with a howling wilderness, could be in greater straits than these people in the middle of "civilization!" "Many…have lost their independence through inability to pay interest on mortgaged farms."—So the debt difficulty of the Germans is not confined to Germany, that vanquished nation; in one form or another it is universal. And America—who is supposed to be at the other pole in the international debt-situation—is no better off than the arch-debtor, Germany herself—if by "America" and "Germany herself" you understand the great majority of people living in those countries.

In the American cities it is no better than it is in the agricultural middle-western and southern states. The *Daily Telegraph* (January 5th, 1931) is responsible for the following account of the marked prosperity of the great creditor-nation of the world:

HITLERIST ECONOMICS

From our own Correspondent
New York, *Sunday*

As January advances the bread lines in the American cities grow longer, and indignation is expressed that the public works to give employment are, for the most part, still in the planning stage. In New York hundreds of thousands roam the streets out of work and hungry.

No fewer than 60,000 persons applied at the Free Employment Agency yesterday for work—temporary jobs in offices, homes, or factories.

Today, as yesterday, "reds" led the unemployed in a demand for greater consideration.

They ask that bread lines be abolished, and shelters be provided where people can wait protected from the wintry weather. The opening of all public buildings and drill halls for sleeping accommodation and the provision of clean bedding and free clothing for children are demanded.

Today Mr. Al Smith, the probable Democratic candidate for the United States Presidency at the next election, asks, "Why should not America know the total of the unemployed—whether it is 4,000,000 or 6,000,000? Why should this country alone amongst the civilized nations not know the extent of the problem within at least a quarter of a million?"

Confronted with these facts, what would the Hitlerist, clamoring for *debt-repudiation* (and America is the main recipient of the Young Tribute, after all), have to say? For if the nation who is ostensibly the creditor-nation is just as badly off (or rapidly approaching that condition) as the nation who is ostensibly the principal debtor-nation, to whom, in Heaven's name, does the "tribute" go?

What the Hitlerist would say, of course, is that he perfectly understands that America, in the mass, is no better off than any other country—but that is after all America's business, not his. He would point out that the conditions brought about in Germany by, first, the inflation, and last of all by the Young-levy, were at least as bad as any other country could show, and in fact more hopeless, as regards the future. If other people did not propose to act, *he* did. And, implicated with this reply of his and used to reinforce it, would be something of a theoretic nature, having to do with the whole principle of debt. And it is to that economic theory that you must give your best attention in order to understand the particular significance of this German movement. For it would not be German if it were not theoretic. And the great impression made by a plausible theory upon a people prone to theory must be taken into count. After all, the farmers of Arkansas do not *theorize*! Yet they are in as desperate straits as are the Germans. If they are driven so far that they *must* have a theory of some sort, they will have to *borrow* a theory—a bad thing, for they have, so it seems, *borrowed* quite enough already. The theory they would borrow would naturally be the communist theory—all cut and dried, and calculated to meet any emergency. They are quite simple people. What distinguishes the Germans is that they have not resorted to this borrowing. They have a theory of their own. It will appear to the average Anglo-Saxon just as mad as the communist. But let us try and get hold of it, at least. Then we shall know just where we are with these lads of Hitler's, what!

Choosing Your Change

 I think I can give you a short-cut to an understanding of the economic position of the Hitlerist. What, in the field of practical politics, spurred him to action, and assured his success, may be summed up, as I have already indicated, in the one-word *debt*. And that word, thus isolated—dominating as it does at once the field of his economic theory, and the field of his political, demagogic, activity—has suggested to me a simple method of approach, as the exponent of that movement. Also, it links up the Hitlerist with many people elsewhere in the world.

 The decade that has elapsed since the termination of the War has been blackened in every country by the shadow of the colossal loan-finances involved in that event. And the shadow grows deeper as we recede from it. On the whole, 1930, with its world-slump, was the worst year of the lot, which is saying a good deal. No intelligent person supposes that we can go on as we are at present. We cannot go *back*. Some violent change in the structure of our present Western society lies before us. Russia and Italy have had their change, each providing a different solution, adapted to a different type of people. The German nation today seems more Hitlerist than anything else. So, we may take it that that is the sort of change that *they* feel most disposed for. And in one form or another that is what they have a good chance of getting. What *our* change will be who knows? It is, as the newspapers would say, a policy of "drift."

 But what is wrong with the present system, that it simply will not work—that at each minute it threatens to break down? It is from your answer to that question that one may most readily predict what choice you will make when it comes to *choosing your change*. If, of course, you are tongue-tied, or brain-bound, and able to provide no coherent answer to yourself, then your change will be chosen for you.—So, what change do you choose? Or have you no will to change at all, and do you abandon your opportunity to make a choice? It is, I expect, the best chance you will get—if that matters.

Now there is a rather odd description or person in our midst about whom very few people know anything at all. I do not know a great deal. But, bored as I always am by orthodox Leninists and good little reds, and still more so by other breeds of radicals—blushing as I do whenever I so much as merely catch sight of a pink fool—I have sometimes been amused by the obscure chirpings that I have heard issuing from holes and corners, and have sometimes attempted to get hold of the quaint motive of their little song. But suddenly I hear this humble and peculiar lay booming at me from every point of the compass!

The burden of this little, highly unorthodox, ditty, I can, I think, transcribe for you. And here it is.

What these still small muffled voices were saying was different from what most people said. Most people, when they considered the present miserable impoverished state of the world, seemed to regard it fundamentally as *natural*. They would sadly reason that *some* must have less and *some* more, because, among any million men, say, there was per day only half a million lumps of sugar to go round. There was a *natural* shortage—or else at least a shortage of a metal, gold, to buy the sugar with. But the pleasant and regular chirp to which I sometimes would listen said *all the time,* "There are a million lumps of sugar *per person*! It is the Golden Age in everything! We live in what is potentially a Golden Age! It is only that tiresome *power-complex* that puts that black cloud over this Golden Age!" So the little inoffensive voice went on and on; and frankly I got sick of it, and never paid much attention. But lately I have thought that I surprised its familiar note coming from the most unexpected quarters—but *in volume,* how strangely different! It is a thunder now.

But I have been using a ridiculous image for this type of person

I have now to drag out into the light and ask you to listen to. He is as a matter of fact far from being a little innocent bird. He is one of the most objectionable and irritating figures upon the world-stage today—or rather he mutters in its wings, he has not even a walking-on part. I hate him.

And what this scoundrel mutters is this: "How is it," he asks, in that even, passionless tone that is to be expected from a demented person, "that, whereas man's technical ability to produce, and to transport great quantities of that produce anywhere that is required, has so enormously increased, yet everywhere in the world today the black cloud of economic disaster and of want—*crise mondiale*, "world-slump," it is called settles down upon every land, more and more deeply and hopelessly? One word—there is only one possible one—is able to provide a satisfactory key to that stupendous riddle. And that word is DEBT! The technique of credit, as that is practiced today—and its sequel in *universal scarcity* and in *universal debt*."

That after all is the "dark cloud"—forever increasing, by giant strides of interest and compound-interest—about which we hear so much in the capitalist press. *That*, and that only, is the "slump"—that is the "trade-depression"—the sleight-of-hand of *the technique of credit* accounts for everything. It is that which—so long as it is allowed to flourish unchecked, like a fearful, invisible, fantastic parasite—must always make prosperity impossible.

One, even (who shall remain, as he more than deserves, unnamed), of these disgusting busy-bodies, in order to describe the terrific financial bosses of the time, has coined the phrase (*coined*, I say—for it is indeed an illicit and criminal thing to do, to manufacture and to pass such a phrase into currency)— "Emperors of Debt."

Now such people as these unworthy and misguided busy-bodies are termed in Anglo-Saxon countries "credit-cranks." As opposed to the conventional economist (of the Keynes type) that is what these revolutionary persons are called. That is because (a) they have found *debt*—and so *credit*, of course—to be at the root of the evil, and because (b) the word employed in Anglo-Saxony (from San Francisco to the Goodwin Sands) to describe a fellow who is no respecter of the rules of the game, or even no sportsman at all, is "crank." It means that the fellow is a screw loose, I suppose, or *sick in the head*. What of course the credit-crank pretends is that where finance, stripped of its workaday bluff, rides naked—except for its (purely ornamental) shimmering golden headdress—he has been caught *peeping*. So he has been branded as a peeping Tom. That is what he says. But how can one believe such fellows? Whether it is so or not I am in any case utterly incompetent to decide. Whether there is anything startling of this nature to be seen, if you secrete yourself and spy upon the fair flaxen lady called rather prettily "finance" (a little like "France," is it not?), I have not the least idea, and have myself never experienced any desire to find out. I am only retailing to you pure gossip—the gossip, in fact, of these self-styled peeping Toms.

ARE YOU A "CREDIT-CRANK"?

———◆———

But are you a credit-crank, by any chance? After all, I do not know who I have the honor of addressing. I hope indeed that you are not, and that of course is what here I am assuming.

It is no exaggeration to say, meanwhile, that finance to me is a closed book. What I know about finance is not worth knowing. I have never had either the aptitude or application required to master even the elements of that strange science. So when I have heard travelers' tales of adventures in this unreal fairy-world of super-specialized credit-technique—which has grown up (unnoticed by the man-in-the-street) like some vast and menacing fungus above the world of primitive, three-dimensional, labor and barter—I have never been able to check them. I tell you what I know, for what it is worth.

Yet I must say this: I have often thought that were I to address myself to the mastering of this dreary subject, and if I became proficient in the so-called science of economics, that I should be nothing more or less than a credit-crank! I know *just* enough to suspect that that would be my fate. And I know *just* enough of these abstruse matters to be able to tell you, in confidence, whether you are a person who, if you went at all deeply into this matter, would be a credit-crank as well.

I am exceedingly glad that I am *not* a credit-crank. To have escaped being a credit-crank is a thing to be extremely thankful for; I found out *just* in time! I said (as I was half-way through a book written by a notorious credit-crank)—"My God!" and I closed the book with a great bang. I was thoroughly startled. For I knew that in another moment I should become myself a credit-crank. And I swore I would never open that book again, and from that day to this it has remained covered in a veil of dust, upon my most inaccessible shelf.

Nothing would induce me ever to touch that book. I am more intelligent now even than I was then, and I know that the moment I opened it and began reading I should probably become a credit-crank on the spot, or might quite well at all events, and would never be able to look my bank-manager in the face again.

What are we to do at this juncture, now that I have confessed my ignorance? I must do the best I can, that is all. It is only by possessing some very elementary knowledge of that order that you can ever begin to understand what the Hitlerist is driving at. And this road via *credit-crankery* is really a very good one—it is a short-cut. I am not the person to enlighten you: but a smattering of *credit-crankery* will serve its turn and put you on the right road, even if it does not take you very far.

What the Hitlerist proposes is, I believe, something *far more revolutionary* than anything dreamed of by Mussolini, who was merely a noisy ice-cream agitator beside these strange fanatics. I don't know how I can avoid saying it (it has to be admitted sooner or later)—yes—you have guessed: Hitler is a B—*Boojum*: Boojum of sorts. The man about whom I have been taking up all this valuable time of yours is *very nearly* what we refer to in Anglo-Saxony as a credit-crank: I am sorry, but there it is. I would go so far as to say that the whole of this Hitlerist movement is, on the economic side, little else but a most revolutionary form of credit-crankery! "*Ein creditkrankische Bewegung!*—Jawohl! Schrecklich, nicht wahr?—*Oh I say!*" as Van Dine would make Philo Vance exclaim, to show how terribly *English* he was.

Credit-Crankery Rampant

———◆———

It would not have occurred to me, as a matter of fact, to have mentioned these ruffianly displeasing Cranks of the Great Credit Heresy, if their doctrine had not recently obtained a deplorable extension. *Credit-crankery* seems everywhere. In addition to the greater part of Germany (and by far the more vigorous half)—and Germany is one of the three great industrial nations of the Earth—also the greater part of the island-continent of Australia is positively seething with credit-crankery of the most obnoxious order. Today the vile thing has assumed such proportions as to be quite beyond the decent limits of a joke. It is no use playing the ostrich any longer: it is idle to pretend that we cannot perceive this tribe of boojums, for they are there all round us at this moment in this post-war waste and—the Sahara of our almighty debts—with entire nations behind them. What is to be done? It is an urgent question.

There are many menacing echoes even in the peaceful and dreamy pages of the *Times*, so agreeably aloof from the harsh realities of this earth, regarding insurgent Australia. There the so-called "Labour Caucus"—the Labour Majority, the supreme revolutionary leaders of the Labour Movement in Australia—are preparing a warm reception for our friend Mr. Scullin, the Australian premier, upon his return home from his European trip. His resignation will be insisted upon, we are told. A first-class political upheaval is predicted for the early spring. The slogan of the Labour Caucus when they go to the country is to be "The People or the Banks!" it appears (the *Times* is my respectable informant). The financial ambassador sent to Australia by England—really it was as a dictator that he went—Sir Otto Niemeyer, was quite unable to do anything with the Australians. He told them quite plainly that they were bankrupt, and he was the unofficial Lord Bum Bailiff, come to sell them up or put them on a graded diminishing pittance. The standard of life must everywhere throughout Australia be lowered, etc. etc. etc. But the "Ozzies" were so characteristically obstreperous that at last he withdrew from the Continent, and the present situation then developed. Wholesale debt repudiation was the least of the Labour threats. On December 23rd, 1930, the *Times* contained the following message:

> LABOUR ATTITUDE TO BANKS
> *Adelaide, December 23.*
>
> A significant statement regarding the attitude of Labour to Australian finances was made yesterday by Mr. T. P. Howard, secretary of the South Australian Trades and Labour Council, which represents all unions throughout the State. Mr. Howard said: "There is a big fight coming in the New Year between the private banks and the people. The people will probably be called on to decide their fate, but meanwhile we hope that the question will be dealt with by the State and Federal Governments."

"The people called on to decide their fate!" Here are pleasant and encouraging words—when we consider that this election is to be run on the slogan, "You, brothers—or the bloody Banks!" Earlier in the year, when Mr. Lang gained a sweeping victory in New South Wales, it was with the cry: "Why pay money-lenders!" that he did it (again the *Times* is my authority). And the South Australian Trades and Labour Council passed the following resolution (*Times*, December 16th, 1930): "We, as the representatives of the workers, refuse to pay taxes till at least the increased burdens have been removed, and all unions will be asked to do likewise."

So much for Australia and her abominable fit of credit-crankery. But something that startled me more, I am bound to confess, was an event nearer home. I refer to that part of the

Mosley Manifesto that suggested *the cancellation of all international war-debts for a generation*—and (most significant of all) the demand for *high wages*! I rubbed my eyes when I saw *that*—and who wouldn't!—for "high wages" (to enable people to *buy* the goods that they and their fellows *manufacture*)—if there is one thing more than another that is the sign that you are in the presence of a credit-crank it is *that*. When you hear the words "high wages" you may be perfectly certain that *credit-crankery* is abroad.

And in the more responsible papers and reviews this was at once thoroughly understood. Sir Oswald Mosley was treated almost as a credit-crank on the spot, though the expression was not used—he was spared that last insult!

"Sir Oswald...believes," said the *Spectator* in discussing the Manifesto, "that under modern conditions the home market must be 'the future basis of British Trade.' All *ordinary people* would say at once that there is not the smallest possibility of enough Trade in this small area to ensure the prosperity and the high wages which Sir Oswald promises. The high wages are to guarantee a sufficient consuming capacity. Producer and consumer, we prefer to say, are to take in one another's washing."

That is the way the credit-crank is always dealt with. "Take in one another's washing"—these are the very words of the invariable sneer with which any honest man *must*, in self-defense, meet the proposals of these objectionable gentry. And you also will notice in the above extract the appeal to "ordinary people"—people, that is to say, who are not extra-ordinary—like the author of the Mosley Manifesto, in fact—not to say—yes, not to say *cranks!*

But I could scarcely believe this of such a level-headed man as Sir Oswald Mosley, with a great parliamentary future at stake. Everyone was astonished as well as shocked, and one heard the expression "political suicide" passing from lip to lip, with shocked, superstitious glances. But when a few days afterwards I was gazing at a photograph of Sir Oswald Mosley in some illustrated paper—there he was standing to attention as stiff as a puppet, clutching his cane, his heels together, with an enormous topper upon his mustachioed dandy's head—I had a sudden "brain-wave" it is called—a sudden flash of light in the darkness—an inspiration of the visual sense. Suddenly I saw it all. "Oh, why did I not see that before!" I exclaimed with delight. "How stupid of me not to have known at first sight! You are a *credit-crank* really—that's what you are! Yes, I have often wondered what a credit-crank would look like in real life, and now I know." And as I continued to examine this dapper top-hatted sentinel, author of the Mosley Manifesto, I said to myself that he looked it every inch!

But if on a sudden I discovered that Mr. Baldwin was a boojum, you will admit that, interesting as that might be, it would nevertheless be somewhat alarming.

It is the very little wistful straw that shows which way the wind is blowing—for the little straw always follows: and if it is to be a tempest the same holds. Mr. T. S. Eliot in his (January 1931) *Criterion* is, on this occasion, the little straw. And (although it would be difficult to convey this to you, I expect) it is a little disturbing to find Mr. T. S. Eliot toying with credit-crankery!

However this may be, here is Mr. Eliot with characteristic boldness grappling with this problem which seems uppermost in so many people's minds. He does not of course say much directly about it, but this is what he says: "We need more and better Economics." Almost with rashness Mr. T. S. Eliot in the relative privacy of the columns of the *Criterion* asserts:

> We need another Ruskin. The trouble with the Science of Economics of today is that it appears in a form in which very few people, if any, can understand it. And, in a democracy, it is essential that people should understand the matters upon which they are exhorted to make decisions, and that they should not be

called upon to decide upon matters which they do not understand. When I read, say, an economic article in the *Referee,* or any of the numerous productions of Major Douglas and his disciples, I am confirmed in my suspicion that conventional economic practice is all wrong, but I can never understand enough to form any opinion as to whether the prescription or nostrum proffered is right. I cannot but believe that there are a few simple ideas at bottom, upon which I and the rest of the unlearned are competent to decide according to our several complexions; but I cannot for the life of me ever get to the bottom. I cannot, for instance, believe in over-population so long as there is room in the world for everyone to move about without suffocation; I cannot understand the concurrence of over-production with destitution, and I cannot help feeling that this has something to do with people wanting—so far as they are in a position to want anything more than food and shelter—the wrong things, and cultivating the wrong passions.... I am not even convinced that the accomplished economic specialists of the Harley Street of finance always know what they are about themselves. I have served my own apprenticeship in the City; endeavored to master the "classics" of the subject: have written (or compiled) articles on Foreign Exchange which occasionally met with approval from my superiors; and I was never convinced that the authorities upon whom I drew, or the expert public which I addressed, understood the matter any better than I did myself—which is not at all.

In the above passage "the accomplished economic specialists of the Harley Street of finance" is going pretty far! (It is rather difficult to convey to you how strong this is, but it is very strong indeed.) Even a *name* is mentioned here—which is more than I should care to have done.

Well, I think I have said enough to demonstrate that there is a lot of *credit-crankery* of one sort and another going about. In some places it is a national issue. That is when (unlike England) the pressure of world-debt, experienced as sudden taxation and the too-rude thrusting down of the standards of life, has brought the multitude out of doors to protest, at the call of local demagogues perhaps or (as with Hitler) some great Parnell-like political leader (Mr. Lang may be that too—I have no information as to the stature of these crank-personalities of the Antipodes).

As to what credit-crankery *is*, if you are not (as you should be) disgusted, you may find that out for yourself—I am not here to teach credit-crankery, of course, nor could I, for if Mr. Eliot understands "nothing at all" upon this matter, I understand infinitely *less*. All I can lay claim to now is to recognize a credit-crank when I see one. That is enough for me.

THE TWO ANTAGONISTIC CAPITALISMS

As regards the financial side of the Hitlerist doctrine, there is no question at all that a violent attack upon the whole technique of credit is contemplated. In their official program that is made perfectly clear. The furious resistance offered to the Hitlerist rush by the republican bosses is largely owing to that particularly extremist credit-policy, which the N.S.D.A.P. has steadily refused to jettison.

Without any restraint, the Nazi sees fit to refer to respectable financiers as *Berufs-kapitalisten*, who (the Nazi asserts) *in ihren modernen Raubritterburgen, den Banken, die Bevölkerung ausplündern*. A bank for these people becomes a "stronghold of modern robber-barons." It is small wonder that the Nazi is not very popular.

Then the profiteer. His exploits would, in the *Dritte Reich*, be punishable with death. *Brechung der Zinsknechtschaft* (the breaking of credit-slavery) is their central slogan. "*In Zinsknechtschaft befinden sich alle Völker und Regierungen, die sich der Macht des Leihkapitals beugen.*"[23] The *Leihkapital* is The Enemy of Enemies. And that is how it is possible for the National Socialists to be upon such good terms with many big industrialists. All proprietorship (that of "the little man," especially as against a monopoly, or centralized anonymous interest) is to be fanatically protected in the *Dritte Reich*:

> Our combating of Marxism, our anti-Marxism, is directed against the state-disintegrating teachings of the Jew Karl Marx, against the doctrine of the class war which disrupts the people, against the

---

[23] "In credit-slavery all peoples and governments find themselves, who bow to the might of loan-capital."

doctrine of the abolition of private property... (p. 38 of *Das Programm der N.S.D.A.P.*)

And, in another small book, the handiwork of the editor of the *Völkische Beobachter*, the principal National Socialist organ, Marxism is described as working in concert with the international Leihkapital:

> *Der Marxismus gab von, den wucherischen weltkapitalismus zu bekämpfen, und arbeitete dock dabei seit seiner Entstehung Hand in Hand mit internationalen Grossbanken und Börsen*[24] *(p. 7, Wesen, Grundsätze und Ziele der N.S.D.A.P.)*

You are in the presence here of a violence of utterance, and an extremism of political conception, as great as that of the communist. Only there is a quite different orientation in the matter of the main objects of attack. Both attack organized society as it exists in the West today. Both attack capital. How is it then that they should be attacking different things, since surely all capital is the same, and all the existing power of organized society is *one*, is it not—and if you attack one part of it then you attack the other?

This apparently is not the case. The secret seems to lie in the word *Leihkapital* or "loan-capital." Also, of course, two people may both desire extremely to destroy a given social system, and yet each may wish to put totally different things in the place of those destroyed.

In an earlier chapter, I insisted upon the fact that Hitler was a sort of inspired *German peasant*. In these particular economic teachings, you have the proof of it, I think. The characteristic interests of the peasant-proprietor, and small trader, are here found written all over these programs of reform and are busily at work

---

[24] "Marxism pretended to combat the accursed world-capitalism, and yet worked from the outset hand in hand with international great banking and stock exchange interests."

in every measure outlined therein. But there is this paradox. It is one of the first difficulties in understanding who-is-who in this particular melee. The interest of the industrialist, so it seems, is in many ways identical with that of the peasant, or at least it can be made to accommodate itself to the latter. That is certainly contrary to what one would expect.

In the political activities of the greatest of all industrialists, Henry Ford, however, you had a startling proof of that fact. For the enemy of Ford (as transpired in his violent manifestoes of a few years ago) was—oddly enough—precisely that *Leihkapital* or loan-capital so much disliked by the Hitlerist. Ford's fellow-citizens at the time said, with a laugh, that they guessed Ford had had at the start, when he was in a small way of business, some bitter disagreements with the banks! That was the explanation, for them, of his behavior. However that may be, you have a strange similarity between what would be the recommendations for economic reform advanced by the world's richest man—that capitalist of capitalists (paying an income-tax, in conjunction with his son Edsel, amounting to £890,440 a year)[25] and the Germanic *Bauarbeiter* Adolf Hitler, whose economics doubtless issue from the fundamental requirements and ambitions of the German peasant class, with their instinct to protect and to increase their tiny capitals. And there you have also at Hitler's side, if further proof were needed, the great German industrialist Hugenberg.

Looking at these plain facts from the outside, as the merest ignorant spectator, there does seem some peculiar and significant cleavage between those who own something tangible (like a farm, large or small, or a factory, large or small) and those who own nothing concrete but whose *matière* is the intangible quantities of speculative wealth—the financier pure and simple—for whom a definition of wealth would be simply debt, as is the case with most

---

[25] Assuming this sum is for 1930, converting to USD and adjusting for inflation would bring this amount to approximately $73 million today.

orthodox economists.

Between these two things there does seem to be a great deal of instinctive hostility. And the National Socialist appears, if I understand him rightly, to regard Karl Marx (and hence communism) as a revolutionary (left-wing or left-hand) representative of the *Leihkapital*, and to regard himself, that resurgent Hitlerist, as the equally revolutionary representative of all that other capital that is work, or that is the product of some concrete act of creation.

It is not surprising under these circumstances to find him drawing up the most ghastly penalties for the stock-broker. Of course, who does love a stock-broker? When people read that the *Monagasgues* have violently protested against the rather overwhelming part that the casino at Monte Carlo and its patrons play in their lives, no one feels great sympathy with the Prince of Monaco and his clients—the *Monagasgues* seem to most people to be in the right to protest. Even more forcibly, who but can help sometimes wondering whether that other description of casino (at the Bourse in Paris, or at Wall Street) where the stakes are the industry and intelligence of vast populations of men, and all that they potentially are or can do—is quite as unexceptionable an establishment as some people would have us believe?—For the most languid economist among us—and I am the world's languidest I am certain—there is nothing very attractive in that stupendous playfulness of Bull and of Bear.

But that is an instinctive reaction merely. I have not the knowledge that is necessary to confirm this with an argued opinion. If I knew more, I might perceive that I had been mistaken. A credit-crank whom I have lying upon my table exclaims: "Can one tolerate any longer a condition of affairs in which the bankers or the stock-gamblers of New York, London, Amsterdam, Frankfort and Paris vie amongst themselves for the privilege of the better pillaging of the poor world?" Oh these credit-cranks! The scoundrel is a bore—it is an old story!—Still, if stock and share gambling *were* stopped, I should not passionately regret it.

I do not feel inclined to condemn a party like that of Hitler because I find out that they would make it hot for the stock-jobber. It is a negative attitude: but at least I do not regard the closing of the casino in the *Place de la Bourse* as in itself either a stupid or a wicked action. It depends what comes after that, and why it is done.

Misery-Spot, or Golden Age?
—◆—

Now as to the Hitler attitude to the small proprietor, or master-workman, or little trader, discussed in the last chapter. In the past I have written a good deal about "the little man" and his ways, and it has been mainly *against* that undersized individual. I have no love for the little man as such. Yet it may be that I did not discriminate clearly enough, at that time, between the different manifestations of his opposite—the great, in short. All that is opposite to the little man is not so very good. Also there are little men and little men, no doubt.

I have no undying hatred for a shrewd industrious peasant. I do not wish to shake my fist at him if I detect him saving money. And sometimes the fellow dances. I delight in the more interesting of his dances; they are very pleasant. I like them far better than a bottom-wagging jazz—which is the folk-dance of the Megalopolis—(gone-"nigger" and gone-underdog for good, choked and gurgling with cheap pathos).

It is the *little megalopolitan* who is, I think, in fact, the worst of all the little men. A really fine peasant is scarcely small at all. There is no one less likely than myself to indulge in sentiment regarding the peasant. But let us give all men their due.

I do not however want to reopen that discussion in this place. All I wish to say is that I agree with much of the criticism of the Hitlerist directed against communism—which has taken the mechanical ways of the megalopolis over into the villages. But especially the Hitlerist criticism seems to me to ring true, when it attacks the substitution, by the communist, of the notion of quantity for that of *quality*. For instance:

> In der roh materialistischen marxistischen Weltanschauung, die an Stelle des Qualitätsbegriffes den rein stofflichen Quanti-

tätsbegriff stezte: welche den Wert der schöpferischen
Persönlichkeit verneinte...[26]

Upon some points, of course, the communist and the National Socialist are in considerable agreement. Ultimately, the reason why their two doctrines could never fuse is this: the Marxist, or communist, is a fanatically dehumanizing doctrine. Its injunctions are very rigidly erected against the continuance of the person. In the place of the person the communist would put the thing—quantity in place of quality, as it is stated above.

It seems to me that in these matters, however, it is a question largely of application. The communist cannot be said to be all wrong, by any means, in his attitude to personality. There is a great deal of second-rate quality or of personality which would be far better eliminated. Where the dogma of communism is bad, in my view, is in its insistence upon the elimination of the very principle itself—of successful as well as unsuccessful exemplars. So, even if Hitlerism, in its pure "Germanism," might retain *too much* personality, of a second-rate order, nevertheless Hitlerism seems preferable to communism, which would have *none at all*, if it had its way. Personality is the only thing that matters in the world. But there is *very little* of it that matters—for the very good reason that most of it is spurious or feeble.

But there is one enormous difference between National Socialist theory and its first cousin credit-crankery, upon the one side, and communist theory upon the other. And that psychologically is I think of the greatest importance. The *Weltanschauung* of the Hitlerist or his near-relation (the egregious credit-crank) is laughing and gay compared to that of his opponent, the communist. The communist world-picture is painted in crude blood-red, coal-black, colors. But if what the

---

[26] "In the raw materialistic Marxian world-view, which substituted for the idea of quality, the purely lifeless idea of quantity, which denied the worth of creative personality..."

"cranky" Hitlerist believes is true, a veritable Golden Age is in store for the world, if only the incubus of *Das Leihkapital* could be removed. The so-called "idealism" of the National Socialist consists in believing that this nightmare can ever be driven out— *not* surely in the pleasantness of life once it were.

On principle—for his is a deliberately catastrophic philosophy (the word is Marx's)—the communist views everything in the darkest colors. Everything for him is *difficult*, and incredibly bitter and black. His is the romantic, the stormy palette. The credit-crank on the other hand (as is perhaps only natural with a partly deranged intelligence) is wildly sanguine. The Hitlerist dream is full of an imminent classical serenity—leisure and abundance. It is, with them, *misery-spot* against *Golden Age*!

Here again I, as an artist, plump for the *Golden Age*! As an academic economist, if I were that, I should, I am sure, be all upon the side of a bitter and dreary struggle for bare existence. For the popular economist, one notices (who is always, in the nature of things, a spokesman of the great financial interests) everything is always particularly dreary and difficult. We may *just* succeed in scraping through the present overwhelming period of depression (he speaks about it as though it were an atmospheric phenomenon, not the doing of men of flesh and blood—that is why his lucubration are named a "science") but only *just*—on condition that we immediately knock off cigarettes, all alcoholic drinks, dog-racing, etc. etc. Rigid economy and *still more* rigid economy, until I suppose we have become helots—and until there is nothing more to knock off at all.

The National Socialist would say, in this connection, that it was only when things were black, and people in great difficulties, that *loan-capital* had its opportunity. Also, it is obvious that communism could not exist without great misery and patent injustice.

The anthropologist employs the term "misery-spot" to describe a district where the barrenness of the soil, remoteness, and other prohibitive conditions, have caused the few inhabitants to become a stunted, animal-like, backward and wretched community. But today, if the present unsettled and harassing conditions are worsened and prolonged, we may expect the whole earth to become, from the human standpoint, one vast misery-spot. Trade-revival, as everybody knows by now, is a chimera. Psychologically, if not physically, the peoples of the whole earth (whether it be China, Germany, Russia, Australia) have entered into the shadow of misery—of mental misery, and in the case of many nations, or portions of nations, of physical misery as well.

Now, in the light of the beliefs I have been exposing, this misery is purely and absolutely *artificial*. It is the result not of an *actual*, a natural, want, but of an artificially-fostered, sedulously-contrived, want. Obviously, there is no real want; there is an enormous abundance of everything, if men's technical power to produce were made use of and put at the disposal of all. But for some reason or other we have slowly been con-ducted into such a state of affairs that, in the lap of plenty, we have agreed to starve. And the science of Economics, as usually practiced, does certainly seem to be there merely in order to confuse us, and to throw dust in our eyes.

The best illustration of how such an artificial state of want can be brought about—and that very suddenly, if necessary—is prohibition in the United States. The untold miseries and absurdities of prohibition need not be catalogued here. What you get with prohibition is this, then: you have the earth groaning with admirable vines, covered with grapes, asking nothing better than to be transformed, by thousands of skilled workmen, into excellent and health-giving vintages. But man (some small group of men, by means of some senseless *Verbot*, *prohibits* this. So there is supposed to be NO wine, or "intoxicating liquor," of any sort! This fiction is embodied in a form of law apparently so sacrosanct that it cannot be reversed, even when it has become plain to everybody that its strict enforcement is impossible, and that its continuance must mean the creation of a particularly wasteful and destructive criminal class, of endless loss of time and money, and danger to the nation's health. But a man-made law must stand, however much men suffer!

Everything is, by human agency, made *difficult*, where everything (if it were only *nature* that man had to deal with) would be superlatively easy.

The sort of argument you will hear from the Hitlerist is this. He will say: The amount of man-power available for productive work in England, for instance, in 1800 was all-told only about the equivalent of what any single moderate-sized power-station has at its disposal today. If this immensely-multiplied power and skill we now possess, thanks to the constantly-perfected technique of industry, were made full use of, a large proportion of the population would literally have no work to do at all. You would have to find them work—hand-industries could be brought back or something of that sort. Meanwhile the dream of the utopians would actually today have come true. Utopian proposals for the "life beautiful" and all the rest of it, would be in full force—*if it were not* for this artificial state of *difficulty* and of *want*. So (say these excellent people I have been introducing you to in these pages) close down the private banks, abolish the ridiculous debts we all owe to each other all round, for all the howitzers and poison-gas we killed each other with ten years ago—release credit, and the most colossally Golden Age of any yet would be upon us. It would be such a Golden Age as man has never either passed through or so much as imagined. *And* there is nothing at all *difficult* or idealistic about it—except that there are a small minority of people who have legal rights over us, and they desire (owing to their power-complexes) to keep us poor and in difficulties.

All I can say is this—if I were to go into this matter at all thoroughly, and if I found that the blamable and unworthy credit-crank had made me dream this dream without justification, he would have to reckon with me pronto: but meanwhile it is legitimate to hope that, although all the ravings of this madman are not to be taken quite seriously, yet there may be *something* in what he says after all. All does not seem quite in order, does it, with the system from which the spokesmen come who tell us not to listen to this crazy optimist? There is perhaps *a chance*. What then?

PART VII
CONCLUSION

Conclusion

I have placed Hitler and his political doctrine before you to the best of my ability, and hope that as a result of this essay the German nation may, here and there, be a little better understood by us. The effort should really be made: for the German destiny is bound up with ours much more than is that, for instance, of cosmopolitan France—which, in any event, is much more accessible to the average Englishman, and so less likely to be misread.

Hitler is not without intelligent support in England. The other day, even, a man very prominent in the social world of London remarked to me that the German, ostracized throughout the world since the conclusion of the war—with a vast class suddenly impoverished by inflation—had suffered from a growing inferiority complex. Of that, he asserted, Hitler was curing his fellow countrymen. Eventually, he believed, Hitler would succeed in restoring her soul to Germany, intact.

Sir Oswald Mosley recently, in the course of a speech at Rochester, pointed out that there had never, in fact, been any democracy in England at all. He might of course have added that there had never been any democracy anywhere. The democracy of the city states of antiquity was government by a relatively small caste of freemen (whose privileges, ultimately, were based upon *race*, as most privilege has been in the world up to the present) at the expense of a helot population. It was an idyllic democracy—for the ruling-class.

Democracy in England (and parliamentarism therefore as practiced upon the continent of Europe) meant merely the Punch and Judy show of Tory and of Whig. For the benefit of the population of England a small, privileged, landed class indulged in a strange declamatory political game (in which fists were shaken and high words exchanged). It was at times highly dramatic, and great actors have trod that model parliamentary British stage. The English people were the spectators—the actors were invariably members of the ruling class. But, for the purposes of the plot, the actors were conventionally divided in two great factions, called Tory and Whig—the latter gentlemen pretending to be in a great rage (or a "towering passion") with the former because they were so very "conservative."

That game is dead and done with—it was over long ago. Mr. Baldwin and his merry men (or rather his very taciturn and gloomy men) is no more a Tory than he is a Whig. How could he be? There is no such thing as a Tory today, in the nature of things—this is not the Age of Pendennis. "Conservative" is indeed a gross misnomer. As a matter of simple fact there is nothing left to conserve.

The Punch and Judy of the Whig and Tory was of the same order of humbug, neither less nor more, as the "dictatorship of the proletariat." The Czar Stalin is the dictator, and he says *"Le Proletariat, c'est moi!"* American democracy is another political facade of that sort. Stalin's democracy is suited for ex-serfs, Hoover's for Anglo-Saxon traditions of "the home of the brave and the free" order.

Under the circumstances, why throw up your hands in horror, Mr. Democrat, when confronted with Mussolini, Pilsudski, or Hitler. If those gentlemen are typical of the community out of which they rise to the position of supreme authority (more or less), that should be enough for you—unadulterated democracy being quite impossible. But in Germany's case a real political novelty has come about: the German nation has the chance at present of *voting* for its future tyrant. Perhaps the German people are today nearer to true democracy, who knows, than any European nation has ever been at all. The English, at least, have never had such an opportunity.

In a book called, in the translation, *Germany and the Germans*,

CONCLUSION

by Eugene Diesel, there is apparently the following passage (I merely quote from a review of the book in a Sunday paper of February 8th, 1931).

> Herr Diesel writes enigmatically of the future: "We in Germany are going through a test so severe that only what is genuine in our economic life, in our intellectual endeavors, in our morals, and our religious and social ideals, will be able to survive. It may well be that the politics of the future will first take definite shape in this troubled land."

That statement, as it stands, seems to me to convey the supreme importance for the rest of Europe of those at present purely German events in which Adolf Hitler is playing such a considerable part.

In the battle for and against Hitler, the fate of his party will be decided upon two great issues, I think. These are communism (understood as a universal panacea) and capital wealth (understood as debt, or as loan-power).

Mussolini only had the former of these two motives to circumvent. If what the Hitlerist calls "international loan-capital" on the one hand, and communism on the other, can mobilize in Germany sufficient resistance to Hitlerism, then of course Hitlerism will be defeated once and for all.

Communism is not in Germany the "party of youth" as it is in Anglo-Saxon countries. Outside of communism, it is true, youth is with us the object of a great deal of courting and ogling, but the seduction is invariably a bloodless affair, and must be, from the stand-point of youth, unsatisfactory. Youth is, with us in Anglo-Saxony, all steamed-up, but all for nothing—it finds itself all steamed-up in a pure political void. It is told how perfectly wonderful it is, in the most luscious journalese—how it deserves everything that it gets, or will get, and more than everything, but at the end of all the pretty fireworks of youth-politics there is youth just where it was before. Nothing whatever has happened—it is merely commanded, because it is so *young*, to vote to put a tax upon the eggs of Belgian hens! *At least*, at the outbreak of the World War, it was hoarsely commanded to go over and sit in a specially-dug-for-it Belgian ditch and have its head blown off—that was more exciting for poor simple youth. But youth as cannon-fodder in the political peace-time battlefield is, in Anglo-Saxony, let down in a very dismal manner—the big guns of party-politics only shoot high-priced British eggs and such uninspiring bagatelles. And, as to communism, in spite of its many excellent notions, it does not really come off with the Anglo-Saxon, or even with the American. So youth, with us, just gets bored, and a force is wasted. In Germany that is not the case.

To summarize this: until an extreme party is started (in England at all events) *outside*, and perhaps in some ways in opposition to, communism (it need not be fascist, indeed it would be better if it were not Italian, nor yet German, in inspiration, of course) to take up into itself all that is most active in the academic youth, and the young ambitious workmen and mechanics, there will be no youth-politics worth the name in England.

In Germany, however, all that can truly be called "youth" is anti-communist. And that is of great importance in that troubled land, where, Herr Diesel says, "the politics of the future will first take definite shape."

As to international loan-capital, Germany is at present the most important enemy of all that can come under that head. But, as I have shown in the course of this essay, Germany is not its only antagonist. Even in the English Parliament, of all places, the other day, the roar of a credit-crank broke forth unexpectedly in the brawniest scotch, and sent a boojum-like thrill through that assembly. The voice was that of Mr. Kirkwood—and since this is the latest outburst of credit-crankery (it is more recent than those contemporary with the writing of the rest of this essay) I will quote it, for I am sure that by this time the reader, like myself, takes

CONCLUSION

some slight dispassionate interest in the manifestations of this inexplicable disease. I cannot do better than quote from the *Times* (February 7th, 1931)—the *Daily Herald* only gave a few lines to Mr. Kirkwood in its report of this debate:

> Mr. Kirkwood (Dumbarton Burghs, Lab.) seconded. He said there could be no objection in that House to the theory of the living wage, because members had fixed the principle for themselves. It was asked, where was the money to come from? Why not do again what was done during the War? During the War they were familiar with "Bradburys." What was to hinder the Chancellor of the Exchequer and those great patriotic and philanthropic gentlemen the bankers from issuing "Snowdens," just as they issued "Bradburys" during the war? (Laughter, and a Unionist Member—"Kirkwoods.") "Kirkwood" was a name better known throughout the British Empire than "Bradbury" ever was. (Laughter.) But he did not quarrel about the name. They might be called "Churchills" for all he cared. (Laughter.) They read stories of gambling by British rich at Monte Carlo. It would be far better if those coins that were passed across the counters at Monte Carlo were passed across the counters of Selfridges, the co-operative stores, and the bakers' shops. There was no shortage of money for the purposes of the Bill. The annual income of the country had remained for ten years at £4,000,000,000, while wages had been reduced by £700,000,000 a year. That was where the money was, and the great reduction in the purchasing power of the people explained the existing depression in trade. He and his friends would continue to use the House of Commons, which he believed was the greatest platform in the world, to press upon the Government to defend the people who sent them there from the ravages of capitalism. If the Government had the will, they had the power to see that the working classes were paid a living wage.

With a few slight changes that could be an address by a Hitlerist deputy—a little more definition (the distinction between *Das Kapital* and *Das Leihkapital* or loan-capital) and so forth. There are your "philanthropic gentlemen the bankers," sure enough (the *Bankleute*), and inflationist proposals in all their nakedness.

But, returning to the prospect of Herr Adolf Hitler and his chances for the office of dictator in the German *Reich*, will he be allowed, after all, to do all these things that he so obstinately proposes, you may well ask—so much at the expense of the vast interests inside and outside of Germany, against which he has pitted his party? It does not, on the face of it, seem likely. But the interests in question have a way of making use of everything, whether for or against them, and Hitler may yet be the master of Germany: one would have to be far better acquainted than I am with world-affairs to answer such a question. Take Adolf Hitler as a symptom, as a point-of-departure, as a significant personal gesture across the face of Europe, as a political hero, as a puppet thrown up in response to an intolerable internal situation, as a Boulangist phantom, or anything you like. I myself am content to regard him as the expression of current German manhood—resolved, with that admirable tenacity, hardihood, and intellectual acumen of the Teuton, not to take their politics at second-hand, not also to drift, but to seize the big bull of finance by the horns, and to take a chance for the sake of freedom.

www.ingramcontent.com/pod-product-compliance
Lightning Source LLC
Chambersburg PA
CBHW021426070526
44577CB00001B/84